Jon Ferguson

The Old Man and the Stone

Musings from Morges

Huge Jam Publishing
First Edition
2023

Copyright © 2023 Jon Ferguson
All rights reserved.

No part of this publication may be reproduced, distributed, or transmitted in any form or by any means, including photocopying, recording, or other electronic or mechanical methods, without the prior written permission of the publisher, except as permitted by English copyright law. For permission requests, contact the publisher.

Unless stated otherwise no identification with actual persons (living or deceased), places, buildings, and products is intended or should be inferred.

ISBN: 978-1-916604-00-1

THE OLD MAN AND THE STONE

May 22, 2020

THE OLD MAN was taking a lovely walk through the forest on the path from the village of St. Luc that winds its way up to the Weisshorn. He was alone and the cool crisp air was already beginning to warm up. It was June and ten o'clock in the morning.

Suddenly the old man came upon something he had never seen before (he had done this hike a number of times during his lifetime). There was a huge stone, as tall as a man, smack dab in the middle of the path. As he approached it, he realized it was even bigger than a man, perhaps almost three meters high. It appeared to be a piece of granite that had probably dislodged itself from the massive mountain above, rolled down through the forest and come to rest in the middle of the path. From the spot where the stone stood, the old man looked up the mountain and saw places where trees had been knocked down or damaged, which certainly must have helped slow the massive rock, finally bringing it to a halt where it now was.

The old man tried to move it, with no success of course. It was granite and it wasn't going anywhere. The path would be blocked for years and years. Fortunately, there was enough space to walk around the stone on the left side going up the mountain.

By noon, the old man was up at the Weisshorn. The sky was

unsullied baby blue and the whole world lay before him so silently and peacefully that for a moment he thought all was well.

THE OLD MAN AND FAULKNER

May 23, 2020

INDEED, THERE WERE a lot of books lying around in many different places in the old man's house. He hadn't read all of them, but he had read most of them. They were on the floor beneath the nightstand and on the fat shelf next to his bed. They were in the sitting room with the stereo system, the chimney, and Miró and Matisse. They were all over the place in his "office" in the basement where he wrote every morning.

He was always fascinated by his literary proclivities and wondered where in his being they originated. For example, why did he read *The Magic Mountain* and *Death in Venice* when he was twenty-four but didn't read *Buddenbrooks* until the age of sixty-five? Why did he devour Updike at thirty-five, but not get through a reread of *Rabbit is Rich* at sixty-nine? And why had he never finished a novel by Faulkner, a writer the Nobel committee considered to be one of the best in the business? There was just something about the way the Mississippian put things together that kept the old man from carrying his torch.

It was the same thing with his love of women, he thought. Some women could be the object of fantasies for millions for men and yet they would leave the old man cold. Others could be considered plain by his friends but had something about them that set his engines to rumbling.

Literature and love were two of the old man's favorite things on earth. While he still probably had a few years left, he wondered if he'd ever pick up *The Sound and the Fury* or *As I Lay Dying* again and read it from beginning to end.

THE OLD MAN AND THE TREE

May 24, 2020

THE OLDER HE got the more he thought about trees. When all is said and done, trees might be the most important living things on the earth. Most people see so many of them that they take them for granted at a very early age, just like they do for many things, including things that are not "things", like consciousness, seeing, and air.

The first tree that really hit the old man right in the gut was the one in the Luxembourg Gardens in Paris that Jean-Paul Sartre described in his book *La Nausée (Nausea)*. The main character stares at the tree and his vision of reality slowly melts away. "Tree" and "treeness" lose their status as "real." Then everything else does too… The old man remembers that at that moment his entire ontological outlook became suspect. And it had remained suspect ever since. The old man had read *Nausea* and *Being and Nothingness* at the university fifty years prior. He much preferred the novel to the philosophical treatise. He found the latter cumbersome and rather unreadable. The novel went down smoothly like warm milk.

When one is busy with the business of living, one usually won't spend much time thinking about things like the reality of trees, what it means to be a tree, and if it is possible for a human to really grasp the essence of a tree (or anything else of course). But when people like the old man have stopped working, their children are old, and they have lots of time to walk and think alone, such questions may run through the mind like music through a forest.

The old man had become fascinated with all trees – not just the big ones, beautiful ones, famous ones, healthy ones, and ones that tour guides or botanists might point out.

Yesterday a friend told the old man that bamboo trees actually have roots that grow to where they know water is and they are so powerful that if you plant bamboo near a swimming pool, the next thing you know roots will push through the cement into the water.

A tree's got to do what a tree's got to do, the old man thought. He imagined one could say the same thing about everything.

THE OLD MAN AND POLITICAL THINKING

May 25, 2020

AS THE OLD man watched political people (in America they call themselves "liberals" and "conservatives"; in Europe the "left" and "right") attack each other and proclaim the rightness of their views, he began to wonder how many of these people had thought through their ideologies back to the two most fundamental questions of all, i.e. What kind of world do I really want? Is the world I want possible?

Do I want a world where all people are financially "equal"? If so, then we must take huge amounts from the rich and give to the poor. In so doing, would we destroy all incentive of creation and "work"? Would the world become a drab place like the old Soviet Bloc? Is enlightened communism possible? Is such a goal noble or infantile?

Do I want a world wherein we all have limitless "freedom"? But isn't freedom always the "freedom" only to obey laws and, if one doesn't obey, watch out? In the end, perhaps only the powerful are free. But even then, don't they have to be careful lest they lose their power to a revolt or rebellion?

Do I want a world where all people are "guaranteed" a minimum of a roof over their heads, food on their plates, and good medical services? What kind of roof? What kind of food? What kind of medical care? Where in the world today are such conditions in practice? Denmark? Switzerland? Should all governments imitate those governments?

Do I want a world where length of life is more important than the quality of life? Should we give equal importance to both? If some people on some parts of the earth are living longer lives than people elsewhere, should we take resources and supplies from them and give to the less prosperous? Who should decide what life is "quality" living? Will there ever be a consensus as to what makes a "good" life?

The old man thought these kinds of political questions were endless and that in the end there were no answers. Did political types think deeply about them? It seemed that very few did so. It seemed that people tended to choose sides on various issues and then berate the other side without thinking through the all the implications and complexities. He thought of issues like abortion and capital punishment, and the very real possibility that no one was right.

The longer the old man lived the less patience he had for political bashing and rhetoric. On the other hand, watching politicians and their followers attack each other was an unending comedy, albeit often a bromidic one.

THE OLD MAN AND THE PEE

May 25, 2020

THE OLD MAN noticed that often the steady stream became a spasmodic spatter. He himself had nothing to do with this evolution. It, like most things – if not all things –, just happened. Seemingly it happened to every man who became old, like wrinkles on the arms, hands, and face, and skin becoming looser on most parts of the body, except the feet, ankles, nose, and the errant-shooting schlong. The latter, except for the greying garden, miraculously hadn't seemed to change appearance in fifty years.

The old man did his best to keep the spurt inside the bowl, no matter how large or small or close to the ground it was. Sometimes he would even get down on one knee to be sure he didn't miss (like when he used to dunk in basketball with two hands so he wouldn't *miss*). In any case, given that his eyes weren't the best anymore (again, not his doing), he almost always took a little toilet paper to wipe the edge of the bowl and keep things in order for the next person, especially if the next person was the woman he lived with.

Naturally, the irregular pee made the old man wonder if a bedraggled prostate gland was the culprit. He had heard so many stories of operations, cancers, pills and whatnot. The last time the doctor examined the area, when he withdrew his index, he said,

"We'll need to keep an eye on it." That was three years ago.

The most annoying new reality was the delayed dripping that sometimes would come after the old man thought he had finished the process of draining the body. A few seconds after zipping and buttoning up, a damp dark circle would sometimes appear on his trousers just below the crotch. Though rarely embarrassed, he still didn't like attracting other human eyes to his woe.

The old man noticed that some days things were much more *normal* – steadier and easier – than others. But, as with just about everything else this side of Jupiter, he was never exactly sure what was causing what.

THE OLD MAN
AND THE WE

May 26, 2020

ONE OF THE old man's subjects of predilection was how the "I" becomes a "we". It was a topic he rarely talked about with others, thinking they would probably not be interested. But the more he thought about it, the more he reckoned it was a perfectly valid question. How do two or more consciousnesses bond together to form a "we" or an "us"?

Every time his mind took up the issue, an immediate string of questions would pop up ... *How strong or fragile was the bonding? What determined the strength or weakness of the attachment? Language? Culture? Commonality? Shared interests? Shared vision of reality or truth? Need? Symbiosis? Parasitism? How long could a relationship stay balanced? Did all relationships eventually become disproportional wherein one side needed or wanted the other more than the other? Did the way people bonded vary from person to person? Did all "we"s have certain things in common? How crucial was the "we" to the mental state of the "I"? In the end, was the "I" dependent on the strength and state of the "we"? Were there "I"s that could exist without the "we"? Would such a state be desirable? Did eagles have no sense of "we"? Did "God"?*

And then that thought would bring the old man to perhaps the greatest question of all: *Were all things linked together?* If the answer was yes, then there really was no "I" and everything was a "we" ... and a very big one at that! If such was the case were we not all fools to use the word "I"?

The old man would then laugh so hard he would have to go for a walk in order to calm his brain.

THE OLD MAN AND THE COMPLAINERS

May 27, 2020

*O*DDLY, THE STEADY *complainers seem to exist in far greater numbers than the happy grateful souls…*

This thought came to the old man as he read newspapers and emails from his friends and watched the news on television. *Here we are,* he thought, *living in the most prosperous moment in the history of the human herd, and most people seem to spend their time bitching and complaining about things. Life expectancy has never been higher. Most of us have plenty of food, heaters, air-conditioners, ovens, refrigerators, clothes for all seasons, soft beds, and solid walls around our homes. Health care is far better than it has ever been in the known history of humanity. We can talk to anybody we want to anywhere in the world at any moment of the day. We can "retire" at age sixty-five, or even younger. We have cars, good roads, electric bikes and amazing airplanes to take us all over the world. We have ingenious computers and iPads and GPSs. We have billions of books and films and YouTube videos. We can even listen to someone reading a book while we take a walk or drive a car. We have by far the greatest living conditions in the history of known humanity… And yet, what do so many of us do?*

We bitch about sexism, inequality, death, Trump, Biden, Pelosi, McDonnell, CNN, Fox News, the left, the right, the size of our muscles and mammary glands, the air, pollution, the planet, pornography, religion, atheists, believers, junk food, the shit on TV, gun control, animal rights, abortion, the decay of America, disunited Europe, dictators in China, Russian meddling, coronavirus, people dying in their eighties, and on and on we go complaining about what we don't like about the world. We have the unbelievable good fortune of *living* today, and what do so many of us do? We spend our time bitching about it.

The old man scratched his head and his crotch. Then he thought, *I guess that's just the way people are...*

He put on his soft-leather Italian walking shoes and went for a morning stroll along Lake Geneva, highly appreciative of the fact that he was still alive and could still walk at a brisk pace.

THE OLD MAN AND THE POLICE

May 28, 2020

THE OLD MAN had defended the police all his life. He had also admired Native American tribes in the 19th century that had gotten along fine without policemen; people policed each other and the only eventual punishment for a screw-up was banishment.

Today the world is flooded with police officers. Unfortunately we need most of them because people steal stuff, destroy property, endanger others, attack each other, murder each other, and cheat in their dealings. Probably a good way to judge a civilization would be a GNP number that stood for "Gross Number of Police", or the number of police per capita. Better yet, a number for the police per 1000 people compared with the number of crimes per 1000 people… lots of cops and lots of crime would be synonymous with a rotten society and vice versa.

The old man was thinking about this because the police killed a man yesterday in Minneapolis. The man was unarmed and supposedly had been suspected of paying for something with a forged $20 bill. He was handcuffed and thrown to the ground and a policeman was filmed kneeling on the man's neck while he was pleading, "I can't breathe…I can't breathe…" He couldn't breathe and he died soon after.

What an horrendous scene. Now people are protesting and

rioting. Unfortunately, in America the color of people's skin still seems to matter and the man who was killed had dark skin and the policeman who knelt on his neck had light skin. A crime is a crime no matter what color the faces are, but this kind of police crime is explosive. The policeman who caused the man's death has unwittingly thrown a stick of dynamite onto the fire of so-called "racial" problems in America. He has sullied the image of policemen all over the land. He prolongs a great American problem.

Had I the power in Minneapolis, I would put any guilty police officer on trial as quickly as possible. I would also point out that officers with light skin have also killed people with light skin and police with dark skin have also killed people with dark skin and light skin, and that sometimes the color of skin has nothing to do with anything, but if it does, it is a very bad sign for civilization.

If the color of your skin influences anything in your life, you are living in a second-rate world.

I tend to agree with the Native Americans: for any guilty parties, banishment is the best solution. To *where* is another problem…

THE OLD MAN AND THE YOUNG MAN

May 29, 2020

THE OLD MAN wondered when the young man became the old man. It seemed to him like there had never really been an in-between stage because it all happened so fast. But then the old man thought for a moment and realized that the obvious truth was that he had never been a young man and he had never become an old man… *Every moment of life is tied together and there is no sense in trying to separate them.*

This thought made him feel better. It was a wise thought. Not only was every moment of his life tied together, but every moment that led up to him was also tied together… every moment of his parents' lives and their parents' lives and their parents' lives, etc., going as far back as back we can go.

So when the old man now thought about how and when he got to be an old man, he realized that he was still as much a young man as he was an old man and that even when he was a dead man he'd be an integral link in a long chain of living men.

The chain of the dead and the living can never really be broken. Neither can the chain between the young and the old. People are just too loggerheaded to realize it.

THE OLD MAN AND THE FLOWERS

May 30, 2020

THERE WERE TWO flowers that the old man had never forgotten. The first was the rose in Oscar Wilde's story "The Rose and the Nightingale". The second was the flower that a Vietnam War protester placed in the barrel of an M14 rifle held by a soldier. The old man thought it was a carnation, the year 1967, and the place was the Pentagon.

In Wilde's story a student is in love with a girl and wants to give her a red rose as proof of his affection. He is desperate because he cannot find one. A nightingale pricks its own heart with the thorn of a white rose, and as it sings a song of love all through the night its blood turns the rose to crimson. The nightingale is found dead the next morning; the boy finds the rose but shows no gratitude toward the bird; when the girl gets the rose, she tosses it in the gutter.

The war protestor's carnation came to mind as the old man watched the protestors smash windows and burn buildings in Minneapolis, Atlanta, and other cities across America following the horrid death of George Floyd who suffocated as a policeman held his knee on Mr. Floyd's neck. A video of the event went viral and the protestors went to the streets. As is frequently the case, many of the demonstrations turned violent, and in so doing had the opposite effect, i.e. they didn't bring Americans together, but rather seemed to exacerbate the "racial" divide.

The same thing had happened in Ferguson, Missouri a few years prior. Then the old man had thought President Obama wasted a great opportunity to get Americans to stop talking about "race" and instead start talking about human beings. He thought that Obama was the perfect person to do that because his mother was a Caucasian type and his father was an African type and so Obama was neither "black" nor "white", but a wonderful mix of humanity – a human being and not a member of "a race". But no! Obama called himself "black" and the racial divide persisted and perhaps even worsened. Now President Trump has a great occasion to stand up and tell people that they are all of one race, the human race, and that the color of one's skin should have absolutely no influence on a woman's or a man's life, and that as long as it does we are living in a second-rate civilization.

The old man was sad because he realized the nonsense would likely continue for a long time and not get better before he died.

We love flowers, cars, cats, dogs, clothes, and sports uniforms of all colours. Why can't we do the same with human beings?

THE OLD MAN AND THE EYES

May 31, 2020

THE OLD MAN thought the two most amazing parts of existence were consciousnesses and eyes. Without them, how would existence reveal itself? How would anything *be*? It all kind of went back to the old idea that *if a tree falls in the forest and there's no one there to hear it, does it make any noise?* Seemingly both men and animals have consciousnesses. How different are they? Could a tree have a consciousness? Or a sun or planet? How does a mouse's consciousness differ from a cat's? How does the old man know that his consciousness works the same way other human consciousnesses do? Perhaps they are very different. If so, wouldn't they have very different views of "life" ... of what there is out there to look at?

The "fact" of the *unfathomable mystery of consciousness* tended to blow the old man's mind, so he preferred to think about the phenomenon of "eyes", eyes that can *see*. See what? What they *see* or what there *is* to see?

The old man wondered how many people question whether or not their eyes really see "reality"! It seems that cats and eagles and other animals see the world very differently from how people see it, and that mantis shrimp see a rainbow of colors that humans can't see at all. But in general we believe our eyes. We trust them with what they "see" ...

O what strange and wonderful things eyes are! So strange and wonderful that the old man laughed at how his own eyes had deteriorated at about the same rate as the wrinkles that began appearing on his face had taken off when he turned forty. Because of this, even at age seventy, when he looked at himself in a mirror he really hadn't "aged" at all! If he puts his glasses on that changes everything. But he only uses glasses for reading.

The old man wondered if he was the only one who wandered in wonderland or if lots of his fellows bounced through life with similar thoughts and questions.

In any case, one thing was certain: people who ask questions about their eyes and consciousnesses are usually more fun to be around than people who don't.

THE OLD MAN AND THE YOU

June 1, 2020

OBVIOUSLY, YOU ARE *as important as I am. And if I dare say, even more so. Your existence is absolutely crucial to you, whereas my existence can only be crucial to you in an abstract sense. You can think about me and how I might feel, but you cannot feel myself like I feel myself, and vice versa.*

So what does this mean? For way too many years the old man had thought about this problem and its ramifications for living. Shouldn't one realize at every moment that every creature one looks at is the most important creature (for that creature) in the whole wide world? When one understands this, what changes in one's existence? Everything? Nothing? A few things?

It was high time the old man answered these questions for himself. Forget other people! He had enough to realize in his own head!

It was June 1st and America was burning. George Floyd got killed by the cops. We all saw it thanks to iPhones and the Internet. No question about who did it and how ugly it was. The policeman whose knee crushed Floyd's neck is behind bars and will surely be there for a long time. At least some quick justice has already been done.

Can anyone imagine what was going on in that man's mind? How much rage must have been stored up inside of him (the most important person on earth for himself)? And then when we watch the looters smashing windows and burning police cars, we try to imagine how much rage has been stored up in their minds and bodies (the most important ones on earth of course for them)! And then when we watch all the mayors, governors, and presidents trying to govern and bring some sense and order to the pandemonium. Wow! There are some serious other viruses and pandemics running around besides Covid-19!

And what if there's no second coming of Jesus, not now or not ever. And hell, there might even be no god anywhere in the whole damn universe. We might really be all alone with ourselves…

Which brings the old man back to the beginning. How do we get ourselves to feel for everybody! Not just the good guys! Not just the downtrodden! Not just the victims! And let us not forget to ask this question… *Are not all the perpetrators of all the shit victims themselves of other perpetrators of other shit?* Doesn't the cycle of screwed up idiocy and stupidity go back forever?

What was blowing the old man's mind was how everybody was simplifying everything as if there were some kind of nice neat logic to it all!… *But man, I'll tell ya… there's been shit going around on this earth for all time and eternity! And obviously there are no simple solutions because it's 2020 and the shit almost looks as bad now as did way back when before Columbus discovered America and all that shit started!*

So if you go outside, don't forget your mask and your shield. And remember, every person you see is more important than you are except to yourself. And they're all doing what they think is right at that moment. I know it's insane. And it is insane. So good luck everybody. And before you go, don't forget to brush your teeth and feed the dog and the rabbits.

THE OLD MAN AND THE BUTTERFLY

June 2, 2020

WHAT DID NABOKOV do with the butterflies he caught? Has there ever been a more sensitive man than Vladimir? Has there ever been a more delicate creature than a Monarch or a Tiger Swallowtail?

The old man thought he – Nabokov – probably made love with them.

THE OLD MAN AND THE SKIN

June 3, 2020

THE OLD MAN has skin all over his body. Everyone he knows does too, but he knows his skin better than he knows anybody else's skin. That is because these days he lives far from other skin. No one explores his body anymore and the only hands that touch his body are his own. That's not just because of the coronavirus, but also because of the absence of love, at least the kind of love where hands explore each other's bodies on a regular basis and with no limits and extreme tenderness.

From his first girlfriend on, the old man thought hands were well used when exploring the body of a lover. Surely that feeling was an extension of the feeling his mother's hands had on his body when she rubbed it with alcohol when he was a feverish child.

It is true, the old man thought, *that there is young skin and old skin. Old skin doesn't have quite the same texture and luster as young skin, but it's still skin.* And yet it seemed that as all people moved from youth toward no more youth, their skin got progressively less attention.

Then the old man thought about people who have leprosy and those at the bottom of the Hindu caste system. Then he thought of cats and dogs and how loving hands caressed their bodies. And of snakes whose bodies he had never wanted to touch. And he thought of all skin-covered creatures all over the world and which ones were the most in need of contact with hands, fingers and other skin.

Touch me baby. Rock me baby. At this stage in life touching was almost as important as rocking.

THE OLD MAN
AND THE MEDIATISED MIND

June 4, 2020

SO, THE OLD man thought, *the American millions – roughly 330 of them coming in all shapes and sizes, colors, strengths, weaknesses and mental capacities – were just getting to the end of the coronavirus saga and were starting to relax, go to beaches and restaurants, and generally enjoy life again, when suddenly a man named Chauvin (a policeman by trade) was filmed killing a handcuffed man with his knee. This horror sent thousands of people to the streets, lots of peaceful protesting, lots of violence and destruction of property, lots of gnashing of teeth, more 24-hour media talk and footage of cars and buildings burning, people breaking windows, tear gassing of protestors, wild looting, and America looking like a nasty place to be. Racial injustice had replaced coronavirus as the new pandemic.*

The old man watched it all from afar, across a vast ocean, where he had spent almost five decades trying – among other things – to be good to all people and, if possible, to get them to appreciate the wonder and complexity of existence.

He felt he had succeeded and failed. There's nothing wrong with succeeding and failing. In the end they are often the same. Each man or woman must decide what counts as failure and what counts as success.

The old man was getting tired of TV. First there was the coronavirus every minute of every day. Then there was the looting and burning, politicians and pundits, presidents, and ex-presidents, sports stars and every Tom, Dick, and Susie talking about what was wrong with America. For eight days straight the old man had not heard one word about what was right with America.

The old man thought that the real problem anywhere – including America the Beautiful (the land that the well-meaning European immigrants flat-out stole from the so-called "Indians") – was stupidity. People were simply dumb. No fault of their own, but people were simple-minded and had little or no perspective on the world. People believed in free will and gods inspiring constitutions and promised lands and grandiose concepts like "freedom" and "justice" that mean nothing in reality but everything in fiery demagogy. People believed they knew what was right and how anyone who didn't think like they did was wrong. People believed they were not part of nature and could be "objective" about things like truth and morality. People believed that existence was something that could be "understood" and that language expressed "reality … And these same people forgot that life was tragic. They forgot that there was insane senseless killing not only on May 25, 2020, in Minneapolis, Minnesota, but every moment of every day in so many corners of this world. They forgot that blaming Trump for racial injustice, police brutality, and racial inequality didn't make much sense because everyone kept insisting that no progress had been made on any of these fronts since Martin Luther King's death, and that that time had included eight years of presidency by a so-called "black" man who didn't seem to help clean up the mess either.

Then the old man thought that he knew a lot of wonderful people of many different nationalities and skin colors who were absolutely fine intelligent human types and who harbored no racial prejudice whatsoever. He thought that the best hope for the world was that eventually there would be more and more individuals like these friends who were blind to color and nationality and understood that the world was far more complex and deep and pulchritudinous than the TV media and mediatized minds made it out to be.

THE OLD MAN AND THE SOCKS

June 5, 2020

THE OLD MAN woke up early as always. He looked at the clock radio on the nightstand. There was a 5, a 2, and a 4. 24 minutes past 5. A good time to begin the day.

He sat up. He felt the usual morning stiffness in his back. His socks were neither dirty nor smelly and he had purposely left them next to his side of the bed on the floor before retiring eight hours prior. He bent his body forward to pick them up. Long arms came in handy. Now he had to put them on.

The hip joint worked okay. His left foot lifted off the ground (*almost like a NASA rocket*, he thought with a chuckle) and rose toward his right knee. He caught it with both hands and was able to quickly flip the open end of the first sock over the toes and pull it around the heel. This was his first satisfaction of the day.

He watched the left foot go back to the floor. He grabbed the other sock next to him on the bed. Then the right foot plopped up on the left knee. He bent forward and caught it too before it had a chance to slip off. Sock number two was in place for the day in a matter of seconds.

As he stood up and went to pee, he remembered he used to be quarterback, pitcher, and point guard. He even used to pole vault. He reckoned he could either feel sorry for himself or realize what a lucky son-of-a-bitch he was to have done all he had done.

THE OLD MAN AND THE TV

June 7, 2020

WHEN THE OLD man finally had enough money to buy one, after two years in Switzerland, he loved his TV. It was an old black and white machine that he put on a table in his bedroom in his tiny two-room apartment in Pully. The year was 1975. The TV was a companion, a kind of friend. It kept him company late in the evening and helped him learn French. On Friday and Sunday nights he would watch classic old movies like *Fanny, Cesar, Marius* with Raimu, and *Les Enfants du Paradis* with Arletty and Jean-Louis Barrault. There were also some delicious Hollywood and Italian classics with subtitles in French. When spring and summer rolled around he would watch Roland Garros and Wimbledon. The ball was hard to see, but not Borg and McEnroe.

The TV had four channels and would go off the air every night, usually around one, and would start up again in the morning about seven.

Today – forty-five years later – his TV is big and beautiful and has five hundred channels and stunning colors, but it is not his friend. His family has it on most of the time, even when they're not in the room. He rarely watches anything, but when he does, it usually sours his mood. Constant horror stories playing out in the family room. Tragedy fuels the news. The more shit the happier the news shows are.

All the anger the old man saw flowing from the TV saddened him. He wondered why all human beings still hadn't realized that every human being had a story to tell, and that all human beings were the most important creatures in the world, at least for themselves. He wondered why something so obvious was so difficult for people to understand, i.e. why respecting the existence of all creatures was so difficult.

The old man thought that televisions often made things worse because they tended to simplify very complex problems and rarely enlightened the minds that watched them. When he watched herds of people shouting slogans he always wondered if they had all been watching the same programs and if herd behavior and mentalities were ever good for the world.

But the old man knew enough to know that getting upset at a TV screen was like getting upset at the rain or a strong wind or an avalanche.

THE OLD MAN AND THE MOB

June 8, 2020

THE OLD MAN couldn't get the mob out of his mind. Mobs always scared him. In mobs individuals ceased to think and let the mob do the thinking for them. This was anathema to the old man. It seemed very ironic that the mob was shouting for justice and the last thing a mob would be capable of delivering was justice. Mobs do not take into account the complex lives of individuals. Mobs do not realize that every life is infinitely complex and that to understand a life… any life… one must research and reflect and dig very deeply. But mobs do the opposite. They simplify everything and hide behind slogans. They lump things together… all police, all "black" people, all "white" people, etc. Lumping people together never gets to truth or reality. Lumping people together is always telling a lie.

Mobs don't "understand" anything. Understanding takes great reflection and perspective, something mobs never provide.

So, what do mobs provide? They obviously serve a purpose otherwise they wouldn't exist and people wouldn't join them. Like churches, clubs, sports teams, fan clubs, bars, cafés, massage parlors, Weightwatchers groups, and yoga groups. Things come into existence for a reason, a multitude of reasons… because somebody wants them and needs them.

The old man thought about the mobs he had seen on

television during the past week. Every member of every mob was there for his or her reasons. They all thought their reasons were valid.

And then there were the police who were there to control the mobs and stop the looting and violence. They too had their reasons to be where they were. And their reasons were valid.

And the looters and vandals. They were moved to do what they did because they thought it made sense.

And then there were the media and politicians. All taking sides and choosing whom to defend or put down.

Where were the voices of the people who were sensitive to all the wayward angels in the zoo?

THE OLD MAN AND THE MADHOUSE

June 9, 2020

THE OLD MAN often woke up in the middle of the night thinking the world was a madhouse. The word "madhouse" brought to mind the word "Funhouse", a place he used to go as a child on the boardwalk in San Francisco where there were mirrors to distort your body and things to roll and jump on. It surely must have been torn down since then.

A funhouse is a place where everyone is supposed to have fun. A madhouse is a place where everyone is supposed to be mad, not in the sense of being angry, but in the sense of not making any sense. When the old man thought no one in the world made any sense, he wasn't being facetious; he really believed it. This was difficult to grasp because the old man knew that 99% of people they make sense, and usually think that it's the people who don't agree with them who don't. Thinking you make sense is a comforting thing. However, when you realize that those who don't agree with you think you don't make sense, if you are open-minded, you must at least begin to question whether or not they might be right.

For thousands of years, humans have believed things that today are mostly considered to be untrue... to not make sense... things like a god or gods creating the world, the earth being at the center of the universe, and Satan making people do nasty things.

But we are still stuck on other ideas that the old man was sure would be thought nonsense in a few decades or hundreds of years. He imagined that the notion of "free will" would fall into this category, and with it, our whole system of justice would be turned upside-down. Even Mr. Harari, in the third volume of his trilogy on humanity, was pointing in this direction. The old man also suspected animals and plants would one day be perceived with greater respect.

The old man knew no one who he thought really understood what existence was. Everybody talked like they did, but he had a sneaking suspicion that we were all full of baloney. Beliefs were fads. Truths seemed destined to turn out to be untrue.

During the night the old man compared how opinions about things were formed before television, radio, and the Internet were invented... even just a hundred years ago! Opinions were formed from reading books and talking to people. Today, one short video can change the state of much of the world. Within a few days, even hours, people have serious opinions about many things they know little or nothing about. This would have been impossible before communication technology took hold of the world. It would have made no sense to anybody to think that beliefs and opinions could change overnight. Today, one viral clip can lead to millions of people chanting the same slogans about what is deadly wrong with the world.

The old man tried to imagine what truths the most sensible people would believe in a hundred years from now.

THE OLD MAN AND THE SUN

June 10, 2020

WHO ON THIS earth do I know who truly appreciates the sun? I don't mean who is happy when the sunlight is nice and warm and heats bodies tanning next to swimming pools or on beaches. I don't mean who is happy when there are no clouds or raindrops on the golf course. I don't mean who is happy when they can push a button and put down the top of the convertible car… No, I mean who truly appreciates the existence of the sun, without which there would be no "life" on earth.

This is what the old man thought about as he lay in bed this morning. The thought was all tied in with the rage and anger going on in his old homeland. It seemed to him people were flat out blinded to the miracle of existence. The sun exists. The world exists. There would be no world without the sun. The sun is there all the time. The earth turns. The light from the sun heats the earth. It seems light is made of photons and that these photons are created by fusion reactions inside the core of the sun. Evidently they all begin as something called "gamma radiation" and were actually created tens of thousands of years ago and it took that long for them to be finally "let out of prison" and be emitted by the sun; then they travel through space and get to us on the earth. We're about a hundred and fifty million kilometers from the sun and it takes roughly eight minutes for these precious photons to reach our faces and fields.

For many years the old man had thought that religions that worshipped the sun made a lot more sense than religions whose gods were abstractions that nobody had ever seen or had truck with. Without the sun, humankind would be an abstraction.

As he lay in bed the old man thought of all the other things that had to exist in order for *life* to be. Water had to be one such thing. He remembered learning in science class that his body was more than 60% water. Don't all plants and animals need water to survive…? So he added *rain* to the things that deserved to be venerated.

Sun and rain. Finally, gods that made sense.

God isn't blessing America. The sun and rain are blessing the world.

THE OLD MAN
AND HIS ANCESTORS

June 11, 2020

THE OLD MAN sat in his chair and thought about his ancestors, none of whom he had chosen, and none of whom had chosen their ancestors. It was obvious: without one's ancestors, one wouldn't exist. In this sense, they were much like the sun.

Upon thinking this, the old man suddenly had a flash thought: *Everything in existence has a similar set of ancestors. For any "thing" to exist there had to have been an infinite set of events that had had to exist prior to the existence of that "thing". This is true for absolutely everything that has ever existed, exists now, and will come into existence.*

The old man dared anyone to find an exception.

As humans, he thought, *we want to go back and find a "beginning" to our family tree. We want an origin. We want to know where we "came from"… how we got started. We want "first causes", "original causes…*

He scratched the top of his head and thought he might have just discovered the human race's real "original sin".

It seems that St. Augustine is credited with shaping the idea of Adam and Eve eating the forbidden fruit and all the rigmarole that followed. Well, the old man thought it was high time we flushed not only original sin down the toilet of bad thinking, but also original ancestors, and eventually the idea of "origin" for everything and anything. Wasn't pretending that things could be traced to a true or actual beginning a key error of all human thinking?

The old man looked at everything around him in his room. Slowly but surely it all began to seethe with infinity...

Now we're getting somewhere, he thought.

THE OLD MAN AND THE UNDERWORLD

June 13, 2020

WHAT IS THE *"underworld?"* wondered the old man. During his life he had heard it referred to as the "criminal" world, i.e. the world of "organized" "crime", like the Mafia. He had also heard the word "underworld" used to mean the place where the dead "lived", usually somewhere "under" the earth. Synonyms include, *gangland, mob, abyss, hell, bottomless pit, Hades, inferno, fire and brimstone, etc.* Antonyms include *heaven, paradise, sky, never-never land, Zion, empyrean, elysian fields, bliss, kingdom come,* and *New Jerusalem.*

The old man thought about the underworld as he watched the NBC *Nightly News*. It reminded him of it. Watching it was like a descent into hell. Almost all of this so-called "news" was about death, destruction, disturbances, anger, negativity, coronavirus, police brutality, and how former military generals were saying bad things about the President. And then there was the President's rival saying his biggest fear was that the President would "steal" the election.

It truly was a twenty-minute voyage into a sort of hell and bottomless pit of fire and brimstone. (*Brimstone*, by the way, means "sulfur", which is the chemical element of atomic number 16, a yellow combustible non-metal. "Brimstone" is also the name given to a certain yellow butterfly.)

Of course, the old man could have turned off the news at any moment, but he wanted to see what 10,000,000 viewers in America were watching on the evening of June 12, 2020. NBC Nightly News is said to be the most watched news program in the country.

In occurred to the old man that the underworld was not under the ground at all. It was in everybody's living room every evening. The old man thought it was interesting to imagine the following: 1) both "heaven" and "hell" were inventions of the human imagination… 2) "heaven" always had a positive connotation and "hell" was a place that was to be avoided whenever possible… 3) interestingly, in today's world, "hell" seemed to be the people's choice given what was served up as the news daily and nightly across the land.

The old man thought this was strange.

THE OLD MAN AND THE VICTIMS

June 14, 2020

WHO DECIDES WHO is a victim? The old man had given much thought to the nature of victimhood. It seemed the world was looking for more and more victims. Victims seemed to be in vogue. Victims seemed to bathe in the tears of sympathy and the press loved them.

So the old man asked the question, *Who should decide who the victims are?* His answer: *Only the victims themselves should have the right to decide.*

But this was not what was happening in the Western world. The media were deciding who the victims were. And their motto seemed to be... *the more victims the merrier.* The old man thought this was totally counterproductive to a good world. For him, feeling like a victim went counter to what made life worth living. Happiness came from feeling in control of life, not being at the mercy of the stupidity – or goodness – of others. Hence victimhood should be avoided whenever possible. The news, however, seemed to be creating victims with a fury.

Women had become victims. Sick people had become victims. People with beautiful dark skin had become victims. Americans thought themselves the victims of Russian meddling. The planet earth had become the victim of $CO2$ emissions. The poor were victims. Children were victims. Animals were victims. It seemed like fair-skinned males were the only group that had not been victimized, but surely that, too, would come one day soon... maybe victims of their egos, or the errors of their ancestors... O life! Weren't we all victims?

Imagine the consequences of such a vision of existence. Instead of praising and exalting existence, existence is turned into a negative experience – owners versus workers, rich against poor, skin color against skin color, left against right, truth against lies...

Isn't everyone debased in such a world? Life itself is no longer a feast of "being". In the name of liberty and justice for all, we have a kingdom of victims who no longer love life, but see it as something gloomy, unfair, shameful, and vile.

But life has never been fair. How could it be? All is in flux. All creatures must eat. All creatures die. The dust of the dead is under every step we take. No creature asked to be born. Nothing asked to be what it is. It is all amazing and mysterious. Should existence be loved or hated? Accepted or rejected?

The old man knew that nothing he thought or felt would change anybody's mind. He knew today's world would continue to look for victims. He also knew that we could all see ourselves as victims of one sort or another... victims of "old age", or even "success". And he knew that those who wear the crown of the sufferer will always be unhappier than those who do not.

No, no one should be allowed to tell another person that he or she is a victim. Only the person herself or himself should declare such a fate... and always with great hesitancy.

Victims give power to those whom they blame for their condition. They take power away when they ignore them and refuse to let them tarnish their lives. And victims cease to be when they find a new path of their own.

THE OLD MAN AND THE MOMENT

June 15, 2020

THE OLD MAN looked out of one window and saw all the demonstrators, unrest, destruction, violence, unhappiness, rage, hate, and suffering. He looked out the other window and saw Lake Geneva, the Alps, flowers, fountains, blue sky, butterflies, his daughter dancing in the garden, and lovely tomatoes growing on the terrace.

Was anything more obvious? At any moment the old man could see the world as a horror show or as a kingdom of beauty. Anyone with open eyes and a human-like brain could do the same.

So who chooses what and why? Do you see the world as a shithole or a wonderful place? Do you curse life or celebrate it? Or perhaps you see and do both at the same time? Do you let the horrors of the world get you down? Do the beauties of the world raise your spirits? Why do you go in one direction or the other?

The old man wondered if most people realized that these options were available at every moment.

But were they really options? Could the pessimist suddenly become an optimist? Could the dark hateful mind suddenly become flooded with light and love? Or rather were all creatures stuck inside their worldview like sardines in cans?

Probably. But the old man saw no reason to lament. Moaning, weeping, and wailing would only add to the ugly side of the equation. He would go for a walk and see where his thoughts took him that summer-spring day.

THE OLD MAN AND THE GUILT

June 16, 2020

WHEN DO WE feel guilty? When we sense we have done something "wrong"… And if we try to do something "right", but the consequences turn sour, should we feel guilt then? If one *always* tries to do what is "right", should one *never* feel guilt? And what about a man – like the Norwegian who killed 69 innocent people – who commits an horrendous act and yet never feels guilt? How should he be treated?

The old man rarely felt guilt anymore simply because he always tried to do what he thought was "the right thing". Of course he knew his idea of "right" was often very different from other people's definition. But he thought he had "thought out" his principles more than most. Could he – should he – have thought them out even more?

He wondered how people's minds could lead them to do things that the same minds later declared to be so bad that a ferocious guilt could ensue and lead them to self-hate or even suicide. Perhaps there is no singular mind inside a human being. Perhaps the so-called "mind" is not a "thing" but is rather in constant flux and evolution just like the "body". Some would say there is a "soul" behind the "mind" and that this soul is the real heart of the person. And if this "soul" is balderdash…?

The old man knew that many people were infested with feelings of guilt. He had had dogs and it had seemed that they too could sometimes manifest guilt after peeing in the house or eating a leg of lamb that had been left to cool on the kitchen stove while the adults had their pre-dinner glass of wine in the sitting room. Can guilt change one's behavior for the better? In the case of the dogs, they had always been "good" dogs, but they did stop peeing in the house. He couldn't remember if they stopped snatching food from high places they were able to reach. His dogs probably had had no notion of sin or evil, but a rolled-up newspaper slapping a nose seemingly had meant something to them and their minds.

Much has been said and written about guilt. The old man doubted anyone really knew what he or she was talking about, other than the fact that guilt was, in the end, always a form of self-mutilation. But was there such a thing as a *self*?

THE OLD MAN AND THE LIVES THAT MATTER

June 17, 2020

THE OLD MAN thought that one day everyone on earth should carry a sign around saying, "My Life Matters and Yours Does Too". Then there should be a sentence underneath the title: *"Is it possible that one life matters more than another? If so, justify your answer? If not, justify your answer."*

Wouldn't this provoke healthy discussion between people of all kinds? Wouldn't it make everyone sensitive to the plight of all others? Usually people are more sensitive to the plight of some selected humans than to others. Can we imagine a world wherein everyone (not just friends, family, and people who agree with us about life, religion, politics, morality, etc.) would stop and take a deep look at everyone else? And what would happen? The deeper one looked, the more one would understand how that person got to be exactly who she or he was. One would voyage into the mind, the body, the upbringing, the experiences, etc. of the other and suddenly say, "Ah! Now I understand why you think and act the way you do! ... Ah! Now I see why your beliefs are different from mine!"

Yes, it would be a great moment of reckoning whereby everyone would begin to *understand* and no one would *blame* or *judge*.

And then what would happen *the next day*, when people

stopped carrying their signs and all had to go back to living their lives? What would or wouldn't change in the world?

Who would have power? Who would decide what and how?

The old man ran his fingers through his hair, scratched in a few places, and thought, *Isn't this thinking the kind of thing the world's top negotiators are supposed to do?*

THE OLD MAN AND THE RACISM

June 18, 2020

THE OLD MAN was sick and tired of the world acting like everyone was a racist. The old man was not a racist and neither were **Charlie Dunn, Will Garner, Pete Collins**. Charlie Yelverton, Ron Sanford, Stretch Howard, Ken Brady, Manuel Raga, Kerry Davis, Sam Smith, Tom Lockhart, Cyril Baptiste, Mike Hopwood, Don Collins, Reggie Gaines, Lionel Billingy, Willie Davis, John Washington, Cornell Warner, Billy Ray Bates, David Brown, Willie Jackson, Theren Bullock, T. G. Bullock, Mathew Bullock, Mike Odems, Curtis Berry, Randy Reed, Joseph Price, Mark Radford, Deon George, Eric Morris, Darnell Clavon, Chris Woods, Herb Johnson, Makita Kasongo, Gino Martinez, Stacy Nolan, Rico Rollins, Hamed Bahraynian, Omar Ahatri, Seyni N'Diaye, Gloria Loosa, Janice N'sambu, Derrick Lang, Jim Cornish, Dulaine Harris, "Snake" Legrand, Simon Breton, Chad Wellington, Johhny Griffin, Harvey Knuckles, Andy Anderson, Manute Bol, Sedale Threatt, Dominique Wilkins, Damien Wilkins, Cutino Mobley, Darvin Hamm, Marvin Williams, Roger Mason, Spud Webb, Howard Eisley, David Wesley, Raja Bell, Pops Mensah Bonsu, Danny Granger, Jared Dudley, Johnnie Melvin, Curtis Loyd, Corey

Duckworth, Aaron Mitchell, Donnie Dobbs, Fred House, Curtis Kidd, Earl Brown, Will Brantley, Lionel Bobesto, Franck Flegbo, Cherif Jordan Barry, Travarus Bennett, Chris Bracey, Emerson Thomas, Kelvin Ardister, and Robert Covington. These are people the old man had worked closely with at different moments during his life and who were supposed to be considered to be "of a different race". The old man thought this to be patently absurd. He had never considered any of these people to be of a "different race! How could they be!!! They were all wonderful human beings that he had had the pleasure to work with and be around over a fifty-year period of living on this earth. They worked together, practiced together, won together, lost together, laughed together, ate fondue, together, chased women together, drank together, took a couple of drugs together, partied together, went to Rome together, slept in the same bed together because they were too drunk to drive home, entertained kids and crowds together, and even cried together a few times. Never ever did the old man consider any of these people to be of a different race. There was only one race… the human race.

And in the year 2020 the old man was so sick of people talking about race and racism that he almost began to hate the human race. *How could we be so collectively ignorant! How could people categorize each other based on the color of skin or the kind of hair they had! How could people be so petty and small!*

The old man had truly loved all the people listed above. And he had loved many people who aren't on the list – because society likes to "separate" them and call them the same color as snow. But the old man refused to separate people into "racial" categories. It made no sense to him. It went against every fiber in his body and mind.

Of course he knew many people had been horribly treated

throughout the history of the planet earth. But he also knew there were wonderful people all over the world of all shapes, forms, colors and consistencies. The same was true with plants and animals and moons and stars and galaxies!

The old man had tried to be good to everybody he came in contact with his whole life long. He had tried to respect everyone everywhere from every walk of life. He knew there were millions and millions like him who had absolutely nothing to do with so-called "racism". That so many people were still obsessed with "race" simply meant that the world was still in a backward state. This saddened him immensely. But he refused to let it drive him to the brink.

In the horrors of the past, the old man thought, *bodies were enslaved. In the horrors of the present, minds are enslaved.*

THE OLD MAN AND THE APPLE TREE

June 19, 2020

THROW AWAY THE rotten apples, but don't cut down the tree. This thought came to the old man as he rummaged through his mind looking for an idea that made sense.

Existence has many rotten apples. Should that push us to reject it? Should the rotten apples become the focus of existence? Or should we glorify the beautiful, healthy, crispy red, yellow, and green apples?

Our minds are always pulled in one direction at the expense of other directions. Some will go left, some right, some straight ahead. Some will turn around and go back to where they started.

When you think of the world, the old man thought, *which world does your mind paint? Matisse's world of beauty and harmony or Goya's world of horror? Picasso's "Guernica" or Van Gogh's "Starry Night"?*

It seemed like most of the people the old man encountered in the year 2020 tended to see a world of ugliness. The old man thought this to be strange because never before had the standard of living been better for humanity. People lived longer, had more comfortable places to live, had amazing possibilities to listen to things, watch things, buy things, eat things, and wonderful opportunities to visit the world, etc. But people tended to harp on the negative. Their minds headed toward the garbage can rather than the flower garden. People will probably claim that they are not looking into the garbage can, but that they are concerned about justice and freedom and such, and that no one should be happy about existence as long as there is no liberty and justice for all. What these people fail to take into consideration is that it is very likely that liberty and justice for all is no more a real possibility than the existence of Santa Claus or God. Hence, wouldn't it make more sense to try to enjoy life to the fullest as one works for – or waits for – Santa Claus, God, or liberty and justice for all?

Let us at least appreciate the good apples as we try to eliminate the rotten ones. But please, let us not cut down the tree.

THE OLD MAN AND THE MIRROR

June 20, 2020

THE OLD MAN looked in the mirror and saw a man, not an old man, just a regular man. But when put on his glasses he saw an old man with wrinkles all over his face, hair that still but was mostly grey, and eyes that were no longer young eyes. He didn't look in that mirror in the bathroom very often, but when he did he was always entertained in one way or another. It was usually when he did his weekly shave and trimmed his eyebrows, nostrils, and earlobes.

But the old man had figured something out that he thought few other people had: *the mirror is not just the rectangle on the wall in the bathroom; the veritable mirror is everything one sees in the world. Everything one sees is eventually a reflection of oneself. No two people see the same thing or scene the same way. Everything we see is a function of who "we" are.*

This is not nonsense; it is deep sense. Imagine a painter, a woodworker, a gardener, a starving boy, and an Eskimo look at an orange sitting on a table. Each will see something very different. What they will see will depend more on who *"they are",* than what the orange *is.* The painter might see color, light, and the shadow on the table (and of course maybe a piece of fruit). The woodworker might not see the orange at all but will look at the table, what kind of wood it is made of, and how it is constructed. The gardener might think of the beauty and wonder of the fruit and the work that goes into keeping an orange tree healthy. The starving child will certainly see something he hopes he will be able to eat. The Eskimo might have never seen an orange before and, having no idea what it is, will be fascinated by this brilliantly colored spherical object... Yes, the "orange" will reflect the person who is looking at it. The orange will be a mirror.

Let us begin to imagine the world, the old man thought, *not as a stage whereupon good and evil are acted out, but rather as an enormous and eternal mirror.*

THE OLD MAN AND THE LABELS

June 21, 2020

MUCH HAS BEEN said about whether or not human beings are animals. No one seems to ask the question the other way around, i.e. *Are animals human beings?* The old man thought this was typical of human shortsightedness. Jokingly he had often said, *To say a man is an animal flatters… the man.* But did he mean it?

The old man didn't care what we called all the creatures of the earth… *"man, woman, animal, queen, king, black, white, pig, duck, worm, porcupine, elephant, rat, goose, or donkey"* … All were part of his overwhelming fascination with existence. Names and categories never revealed the reality of anything. In fact, they tended to do the opposite and make things "ordinary". But nothing was ordinary.

Forget names and categories, the old man thought, *and instead look at what each creature does. First, admire that fact that it "does" anything at all: admire the force… the will… the energy that pushes it on and on until it acts no more. Then look at how the creature affects the other parts of the universe around it, for better or for worse, depending on which eyes are looking. O life! O world! Labeling all your parts seems to often be the "human" way of putting "people" on a paltry throne. But there is no throne in the Kingdom of Infinity.*

THE OLD MAN AND THE C

June 22, 2020

THE OLD MAN ruminated about the letter "c". Why would it sometimes be used as an "s" sound and sometimes as a "k" sound. Why would an alphabet come up with such a letter?

It seems the Roman, Greeks, Phoenicians (here the "c" is a "sh"…), and Etruscans (here it is a hard "k"…) all had something to do with the "c" the English alphabet finally ended up with. The old man wouldn't dare try to trace the origin of such a complex history that goes back thousands of years. But he would dare ask why languages took themselves so seriously. Of course he meant: *Why do "people" take their languages so seriously?*

In English there are twenty-six letters. The Hebrew alphabet has 22, Arabic 28, Greek 24, Etruscan 20, Latin 21, and a Slavic alphabet has 40. And the Khmer (Cambodian) alphabet is the champion with 74 letters. Of course languages like Chinese have no alphabet per se, but rather thousands of pictographs to get across what they want to say.

The old man wondered which language – and alphabet or pictures – might be the best at describing the "real" world. But then he knew that was a silly thought, so he decided to ask a couple of questions he didn't think were silly: *Does any language NOT claim to describe reality? Is all human thinking limited by the language one is thinking in? Do languages obscure truth more than they reveal it?*

Thinking about the letter "c" was a good way for the old man to start the day. How could one get too serious about anything when all languages looked – and felt – like a kind of metaphysical quicksand? Fickle inventions of human – *all too human* – minds.

THE OLD MAN AND HAYDN'S 103RD

June 23, 2020

WHEN THE OLD man put on Haydn's Symphony No. 103 ("Drum Roll"), the world – according to all news outlets he had read or watched lately – was in a state of great turmoil. The coronavirus was making a comeback, protesters were tearing down statues of old American heroes, Stuttgart had been the scene of street violence and looting the night before, Trump and Biden were being made to be absolute fools depending which side of the press you were looking at. Yes, according to the news, the world was falling apart.

Hence, when the old man got in the car, he didn't turn on the radio. Instead he reached behind him and with a long arm grabbed a CD on the floor of the back seat. It just happened to be Haydn's 103rd. He popped it in the slot. (He was still in the CD generation.) Within seconds life felt good again. What sound! What beauty! What harmony! All the people and instruments coming together to create glorious… music!

The old man thought about world civilization and all the incredible things great minds had come up with. In a few short thousands of years, humanity had gone from living in mud and grass huts and beating tom-toms to Vienna, Paris, Venice, Haydn, Mozart and Beethoven. And then came the 19th, 20th, and 21st centuries and the great industrial revolution.

And here we are today. Many people say we are at a "turning point". What kind of turning point? the old man wondered. Where will the cries of liberty and justice for all take us this time? Will power fall into fresh hands? If so, how will they use it? After we pull down statues of Teddy Roosevelt and George Washington, who will be put up in their places?

If the old man knew one thing it was that power decides what is "right". If power doesn't like termites, it gets rid of them. If power thinks people should stay inside when the coronavirus strikes, people stay inside. If power says people can go outside, they go outside.

He also knew that passion decides what is beautiful. Haydn's 103rd was beautiful. He knew it.

But he knew too that not everybody's passions were the same. He hoped power and passion would let Haydn live a little longer – at least while his grandkids were bustling about.

Before he got home he thought about something else. *Music has a big advantage over literature: You don't have to speak German to listen to Haydn. He never needs to be translated…*

And the drums rolled again.

THE OLD MAN
AND THE STATUES

June 24, 2020

YES, DEMONSTRATORS ACROSS America were tearing down and desecrating statues – not just those of Southern generals, but also monuments of people like Ulysses Grant, George Washington, and Teddy Roosevelt. Even Christopher Columbus got dragged through the streets of Virginia, spat on, and burned. In England, Winston Churchill and Edward Colston had come down. King Leopold II of Belgium, who made the Congo his second home, was also biting the dust.

As his eyes watched this unfold, the old man's mind wandered in many directions. First, he wondered if the demonstrators had any thought for the artists who spent hundreds and hundreds of hours creating the sculptures. Surely not. Then he wondered why it had taken so long for people to understand that the world was not a moral place and that conquerors were also destroyers. Had it taken these rioters five hundred years to realize that Columbus wasn't a saint? Had they never understood that America had been founded on the destruction of various civilizations? Had they heretofore not noticed that kings and presidents and generals tended to live rather luxuriously while millions of others often labored for menial wages or simply room and board?

He wondered what human being would – or could – be unanimously considered deserving of statue status?

Then his mind meandered to other statues that he feared might come down soon. Would the Venus de Milo get lassoed and pulled down to the floor in the Louvre by individuals or groups who were offended by the bare breasts or color? Would the statue of David meet a similar fate at the hands of Puritans who were galled by visible male genitalia? Shouldn't Native American groups want to see the Statue of Liberty demolished? In the end, didn't all those poor and persecuted Europeans who came across the ocean in the 18th and 19th centuries confiscate almost all their land and treat the native "Americans" worse than slaves? (He wondered who they – the Native Americans – might have stolen it from…) And surely all Ronald McDonald statues would one day encounter the wrath of militant vegetarians…

The old man scratched his head and again thought about how little perspective most people had on their own lives and the lives of others. People were people – generally so simple and naïve. But the old man was tolerant because he knew no one asked to have the mind he or she had, including the old man himself. He decided he would change scenery for a while and take a walk along the lake. Such brisk strolls often inspired contemplations about mystery and magnitude and made him forget about fatuity and foolishness, though maybe in the end all were in the same basket.

THE OLD MAN AND THE STATUE IN RIO

June 25, 2020

WOULD THEY GET *the statue in Rio de Janeiro? Who are "they"? On what grounds would "they" topple it?...* The old man wondered this morning.

Who were *"they"*? *They* were the people around the world these days that thought they had the right to tear down public statues and were doing so. *They* seemed to consider *them*selves morally superior to the dead people whose statues they were destroying.

Would they go after Jesus one day? The old man wouldn't put it past them. People who considered themselves to be the beacons of moral goodness would go to great extremes to protect themselves and/or spread their cause. These people came from all sides of the political spectrum. Some – like Genghis Khan, Alexander the Great, Tamerlane, Attila the Hun, Augustus Caesar, Charlemagne, and Adolf Hitler – wanted to conquer the world. (Perhaps some religious groups might be thrown in here, too.) Others – like Lincoln, Churchill, Roosevelt, Truman, Stalin, and Eisenhower – thought they had the best form of government and "good on their side" and would go to war, and even drop atomic bombs, to protect their vision of the world. Obviously, most of us were happy that these men had done what they did. Nonetheless, probably all statues honoring these people could eventually become prey to moral supremacists.

So what about Jesus? the old man wondered as he sat in his favorite chair. Was the statue in Rio not the greatest symbol of the Christian faith? If it were to be toppled, all statues of Jesus might meet the same fate. What could Jesus be linked to that might incite the wrath of today's demonstrators?

Actually the old man could think of many things. For a start, weren't the demonstrators calling for "freedom" and "justice" *for everyone*? Hence, they could strike anywhere they saw "unfreedom". Christianity – the world religion named after Jesus Christ, the so-called *Son of God Himself* – could easily be attacked for being a religion of slavery. The Founding Fathers were mostly "Christians" who had slaves. Perhaps more importantly, Christianity could be said to "enslave the mind". Don't all "hard" religions that dogmatically claim to be "the truth" preclude all other religions from that status? … Hence, down with all the statues of Jesus!

Of course this was an absurd simplification. Of course the demonstrators themselves had minds that were enslaved by other forms of simplistic thinking. Of course they were more than likely just as guilty (or even more so) as religions of enslaving minds with untruths and gross simplifications of history and reality (whatever that was).

Yes, Jesus could come down. But so could just about everybody else who had walked the face of the earth.

The old man had always thought Jesus was probably a very nice guy. As a child he had even tried to emulate him. Of course he later realized that no one really knew the real Jesus. But no one really knew the real nature of anybody, including the people whose statutes were getting knocked down. People who thought deeply about these things didn't tear statues down, didn't want to conquer the world, and didn't think they were morally superior to everybody else. They just tried to be respectful and kind to as many people as possible. But there were limits. The old man wondered who knew best what those limits were…

THE OLD MAN AND THE MEMORY

June 26, 2020

How, THE OLD man thought, *could anybody trust her or his mind?* He had just received some old newspaper clippings from a friend about a basketball game he had played and coached in 1985. His team had beaten the Swiss champions and he had made a couple of big baskets at the end of the game. The old man had absolutely no recollection of the game. Zero. Niente. Nada de nada. His own mind had forgotten everything as if he had never been there. But there was a photo of him shooting from the corner to prove his mind was amiss.

The old man had thought many times: *The mind is a selective sieve. Some things stick and we have no idea why. Other things disappear and we have no idea why. In any case, all memories are partial and fragmented. In every second of every life, one is surrounded by a context that gets chopped to smithereens by the mind. Only bits and pieces are remembered. There is no guarantee that even the greatest mind can ever have an actual "true" memory of anything...*

The old man's mind was flying like a flock of birds on hearing a gunshot. How amazing consciousness was! How amazing life was! He felt the flow of being like a cosmic tsunami. He knew the moment would soon be a memory, and a moth-eaten one at that.

THE OLD MAN AND THE PRINCIPAL ASCERTAINMENT

June 27, 2020

AFTER SEVENTY YEARS of living and fifty-two years of thinking, the old man's principal ascertainment of human beings was that essentially all were enslaved by the world into which they had been thrown. Here the word "enslaved" was not intended to have a negative connotation, as in "forced" labor, but rather indicated that people were slaves to their situations, i.e. they were incapable of thinking "freely", outside the boundaries of their time and place. All were enchained by the social, political, and ontological verities of their time.

The old man thought a good metaphor might be that all were fish in the sea and few, if any, were able to jump out of the water and crawl on land and gaze at the open sky, the sun, and the rest of the universe.

The ocean stretched around the globe, and the fish remained fish and they remained prisoners of the water. Open air and the celestial expanses were for creatures of a different sort. There were fish of all kinds – bristle mouths, cod, tuna, whales, sharks, eels, bass, crabs, stingrays, jellyfish… billions and billions of them… but *fish* nonetheless that were incapable of realizing that they were all prisoners of the ocean.

The old man did not think it was bad to be a fish. Being a fish was certainly better than being nothing at all. But as he grew older, he tired of swimming all the time, and watching others swim. He had begun to feel the weight of the water pushing on him from all sides. He dreamed of flying above and beyond the ocean… to where he did not know.

THE OLD MAN AND FERGUSONIAN BLISS

July 1, 2020

WHEN THE OLD man was young he used to mostly look at young people. They were more his style and easier to look at than old people who were wrinkled, greyish, stooped, slow, and often wore old-fashioned clothes. The young old man liked his grandparents and Aunt Rilda (a great-aunt who brought popcorn every Thanksgiving and Christmas), but that was about it. Old people were to be polite to and maybe helped across the street, or sometimes you might carry a grocery bag for them or go to their funeral when they died.

Now that the old man was an old man he looked at old people more than young people. He was fascinated how each had his or her way of getting old. Some were really old like the ones he saw when he was young. But there were others who looked like they were still rather young, but they weren't because they were old. When you're old you can't be young, except in mind.

Actually, the old man thought the secret to life was not seeing it in terms of opposites. There was no up or down in the universe. No high or low or big or small or young or old. It was all relative. *But relative to what?* Was the universe young or old? Was the universe big or small? Was mankind the only creature in the universe that cared about such things?

As the old man thought about this he no longer felt old. He

didn't feel young either. He decided that from now on he would throw the old-young dichotomy out the window. He would also toss out the theory of relativity because if there were no absolutes (and things were only relative to each other), then it made no sense to talk about near or far, old or young, intelligent or stupid, white or black, rich or poor, tall or short, or even dead or alive. No! These were all human-made inventions that kept humankind in an enslaved state of mind. The shackles would fall away when minds were able to see past the worn-out dichotomies and into the freshly-cut fields of fergusonian bliss.

THE OLD MAN AND THE LAKE

July 2, 2020

THE OLD MAN lived on a lake, Lake Geneva. All the Swiss, except people from Geneva, call it *"Lac Leman"*. The people from Geneva call it *"Lac de Genève"*, which may or may not tell you something about the people of Geneva.

Lac Leman is a big lake that is shaped like a boomerang or a slice of cantaloupe. When he first came to Switzerland, the old man often jogged along its shores or sat on a bench near the water to read, reflect, or see. He loved the light that made the lake glitter and the whisper of the water when it rolled against the pebbles or sand near his feet. He was also fascinated by how the lake was always a different color depending on the season, time of day, and whether or not there were clouds above it.

The old man still often took walks along the lake. The last time he did so, he realized how little he knew about what was *inside* the lake. All he ever saw was the surface. There was a whole living world inside the lake that he knew nothing about… absolutely nothing except for the names of a few fish that lived therein and sometimes appeared on a dinner plate.

He had thought there was an extrapolation to be made: Our eyes see the surface of *everything*. Yes, we might peel off a layer here and there, but we are always on "the surface". Try as we may, we can never see anything for what it really and truly is. Oh yes, one can dive in the lake (or one can cut open a cantaloupe). But one's eyes will always be looking at another surface and one's body will always remain separated from the water.

Switzerland has hundreds of lakes. Seemingly they warm the hearts of strollers of all ages, sizes, colors, backgrounds, and political, religious, ethical and epistemological leanings.

THE OLD MAN
AND THE FOURTH JULY

July 4, 2020

THE OLD MAN imagined how different people would feel differently about the 4th of July American Independence Day celebration...

The Indians would still be pissed off.

His brothers Tom and Larry would be proud of their country and would probably fly a flag in their front yard. They believed God inspired the Founding Fathers and that God blessed America.

His sisters Jennie and Sherilee would most likely have mixed feelings because they had their doubts about the existence of an Almighty God and they realized America was founded on the theft of land from the native people and the importation of slaves from Africa. Yet they did enjoy a good meal and fireworks.

Black Lives Matter people would be thinking the 4th of July should be more a day of mourning than celebration. Their minds would be homing in more on the negatives of life than the blessings.

His Aunt Betty never liked holidays of any kind because when the family got together she always felt like she had gotten the short end of the stick and was never happy. She died thirty-five years ago and as far as the old man knew she was still dead.

The old man had been to Mount Rushmore (where President

Trump was going with his wife Melania to celebrate the holiday) and had thought often about the irony of the Black Hills (given to the Indians by the U.S. government, then taken back after gold was found therein) being the home for the gigantic granite faces of Washington, Jefferson, Lincoln and Roosevelt. He had seen the film "Little Big Man" many times and had thought it to be one of the most intelligent films ever made.

The 2020 4th of July celebration would surely be a special one for many people in the United States of America. Not only had the Black Lives Matter movement reached a crescendo with the George Floyd killing, but Covid-19 was battling for new media headlines with more force and durability than anything the old man had ever seen. He himself hadn't celebrated Independence Day more than any other day for the last fifty years. Neither had his dogs, cats, and children.

THE OLD MAN AND THE OLDER MAN

July 7, 2020

ONE BEAUTIFUL SUMMER day two old men were sitting on a terrace overlooking Lake Geneva. One asked the other where Mt. Blanc was. On a clear day it would have been perfectly visible from where they were – the Aubonne Hospital. The day was sunny and warm, but there were Hodleresque clouds draped along the Alps. "It's right there," the younger old man said pointing a finger across the lake. "You can see snow there on the lower part, but the top of the mountain is behind the clouds." The older old man had a neck brace on which made following the finger a bit arduous. He had fallen down some stairs while going to fetch a bottle of white wine in his poorly lit cellar seven weeks prior. He never got the bottle and instead got six cracked ribs, a broken collarbone, and a fractured spine. Aubonne was his third hospital. *It was half old folks' home* and half *hospital specializing in long-term recovery*. The two old men were drinking apple juice.

"Do you remember anything about the fall?" the younger one asked.

"No, nothing…"

The younger old man didn't push his friend because he knew that when he fell he had been very intoxicated. They had often drunk white wine together in the gallery or the garden. Had the younger old man been there, he never would have let his friend go get that bottle of wine. The just-one-more bottle was usually one too many.

He asked, "Do you often think about the gallery?"

The old man's eyes opened a bit wider. He sipped his apple juice and pondered. Both men sensed there might never be another show. The older man was almost eighty and before falling had had a number of health issues. There hadn't been a show for more than six months. The younger old man had been part of that last show.

"Not much," the older man said.

The Gallery Roch was the biggest and most beautiful gallery in the area. It had prospered for thirty-five years. When the old man was young he had converted an old farmhouse into a gallery in the small village of Ballens at the foot of the Jura Mountains. All the top painters in the area had wanted to exhibit there. Many had. Many were now dead. Over the past decade, keeping a gallery alive had become increasingly difficult.

"Have you had many visitors here in Aubonne?"

"No. Adelaïde came two days ago with the neighbor." Adelaïde was the woman he lived with. She was older than he was. They often fought. The younger man thought fighting was their glue, as for Elizabeth Taylor and Richard Burton in *Who's Afraid of Virginia Wolf?* Burton was buried in Céligny, only twenty kilometers away. The young old man had visited his grave forty-seven years prior when he first came to Switzerland.

"How is she doing?"

The older man ran his fingers through his long grey mane. She had been worse off than he was before he fell down the stairs. She had been spending almost all day on the couch with the TV on, hardly eating, mostly drinking. The house was connected to the gallery. She would rarely make it from one side to the other.

When she did, it was usually to start an argument with whoever was in the gallery. Both of the old men had often been targeted. She was by no means a cruel person. She had had a very difficult life that had soured some with time.

"She's okay. A woman comes three times a week to check on her."

There were two other patients on the terrace. One was alone and smoking a cigarette. She seemed perfectly happy. The other looked like his coffin was waiting for him. His head drooped and he spoke hardly a word to his two visitors, probably his wife and daughter.

"I don't think I've had a glass of apple juice for ten years," the younger old man said. The older man smiled. When the younger old man asked if he missed the white wine he said, *"Non, pas de tout."*

The younger old man thought that were he a god, he would have divined that in the case of the man across the table with a brace on his neck, the beautiful vineyards – that lay in front of them like a glorious tablecloth over the lakeside land – were both the problem and the solution.

THE OLD MAN AND THE STUFF AROUND HIM

July 8, 2020

WE ARE ALWAYS *surrounded by piles of stuff… Even air is 'stuff'… we just can't see it,* the old man thought as he sat in his messy office and looked around. At the same time, everything seemed very heavy and very light. He felt crushed by the weight of the clutter and concomitantly felt it could all fly away. This was how the old man liked it. He had once written, *Either everything is sacred or nothing is sacred. Which is it?* Machines, books, pictures, manuscripts, rugs, stacks of papers, boxes of junk – all were pushing in on him from all angles. *Here I am… in the middle of it… But one is always in the middle of it… There was no escaping it. One way or another, the weight of the universe is always pushing in on all of us and from all sides. We simply don't feel it, like fish don't feel water.*

The old man realized that nothing was "alone". One might feel alone, but one was always in the midst of *Being*, sometimes crushed and other times soaring.

THE OLD MAN AND THE SOUND OF THE POPPING CORK

July 8, 2020

RECENTLY, THE OLD man had been listening to all his old CDs, primarily symphonic music. Everything he heard made his body shiver. Beethoven, Brahms, Bach, Bernstein, Schubert, Schumann, Haydn, Mozart, Tchaikovsky, Rachmaninoff, Copland, Fauré, Massenet, Debussy... All had composed incredible music that was played by orchestras, recorded by other human beings, and then delivered to him via the CD player in his car or living room. Having this happen – having such an opportunity and good fortune – was unheard of a hundred years ago. Then you had to be in the concert hall to hear such music. Today, we can hear it anytime... anywhere. We are such lucky ungrateful bastards.

The old man usually listened to the same piece three or four times in a row. Each time he was even more amazed by the complexity of the sound and the genius of the composer. Then he would move on to another piece. And another. And another. What sound! What music!

There was a different heavenly sound that also made the old man quiver. It was the sound of the cork popping out of a wine bottle. Every time he heard it, it too sent a frisson through his body. It meant a moment of calm, sensuality, and celebration. It meant wine would soon be touching lips and tongues and seeping down the gullet and into blood and brains.

Music and wine gave sparkle to the old man's existence. Winemakers were also composers to be honored and revered. Their symphonies flowed from the bottle after the corks had sounded the first note.

THE OLD MAN AND LONGFELLOW

July 11, 2020

THE OLD MAN sent the piece about Mike Tyson to his son, Jackson, a man with the gentlest of hearts. The son responded with a quotation from Henry Longfellow: *If we could read the secret history of our enemies we should find in each man's life sorrow and suffering enough to disarm all hostility.*

The old man used to say, *"If I were you, I'd be just like you."* Yes, if we knew the real *total* "truth" about the life of any creature on earth, it would be very hard to hate that creature. Perhaps dislike or disagree with, but not hate.

But given that we can never know that "truth", the old man ruminated, *we are left with two possibilities: Either we learn to hate or we learn to love.*

He reckoned that was what his son was trying to say.

THE OLD MAN
AND FAULKNER: PART TWO

July 23, 2020

IT FINALLY HAPPENED. Better late than never, they say. The old man read *As I Lay Dying* from beginning to end. It occurred on a vacation to Nice, France. He read it on the beach between swims in the Mediterranean Sea, on park benches, and in the hotel bed in the middle of the night. It was a book he wouldn't forget… like *The Magic Mountain, The Plague, Nausea, L'éducation sentimentale, The Stories of John Cheever, The Gay Science, Twilight of the Idols,* or his own book, *Farley's Jewel.* He mentioned his own book not to pat himself on the back but because it was a book that had followed him through life. Many books were quickly forgotten. This would not be the case with *As I Lay Dying*.

A great book, the old man thought, *is one that makes one feel existence to the bone*. How does one feel existence to the bone? Of course this was a very tricky question, one that perhaps had no answer. Or maybe it had a different answer for every thinker on this earth. In *As I Lay Dying*, the reader sees the death of Addie Bundren through the eyes of 15 different characters. As one reads, the person who comes closest to *feeling life to the bone* is the son Darl. In the end he gets carted off to a mental hospital.

As far as the old man knew, Faulkner himself never spent time in a mental institution. *On the other hand*, the old man thought, *maybe Faulkner thought he was born in an asylum and never left.*

THE OLD MAN AND LIFE BEFORE DEATH

July 26, 2020

THE OLD MAN had long ceased to worry about the conundrum of what happens after one dies. A *quoi bon* to preoccupy oneself with something about which one has no clue. The same goes for wondering where one might have been – or not been – before birth. Hence, the old man decided many moons ago that the only thing that he should rightfully concern himself with is what happens during life before death. His thought: *Life before birth? Doubtful and total mystery. Life after death? Doubtful and total mystery. Life after birth and before death? Feels real and more or less sufferable.*

So, what was happening *on this day before death?* It was eight-thirty in the morning on a Saturday (at this stage in life it made very little difference what day it was). He was in his chair, like every morning, breathing, thinking, writing, not knowing what feeling, sensation, or thought would come next. Some he would write down, others he wouldn't.

As he breathed, thought, and wrote, he was listening to music. First there was Hvorostovksy and Kaufmann singing the "Fishers' Duet" from Bizet's *Les Pêcheurs des Perles*. The idea for doing this came to him after talking to three old high school buddies on a Zoom call and discovering that he and Bill Milton had fallen in first-love with the same girl in high school. The duet always sent shoots of whatever-it-was up his spine and life felt like a sensational phenomenon. He thought Hvorostovsky and Kaufmann were perfect for the duet. As he listened he remembered that Hvorostovsky was dead. He would never have another day (like the old man was having) of life before death. A silly brain tumor killed him at fifty-five. As the old man watched Hvorostovsky perform, he wondered how many women the charismatic singer had made love with before he died (he seemed profoundly heterosexual), and how he and the women felt while it was happening. This sent his mind packing and thinking about ecstasy, romanticism, and what made life worth living. He knew he himself was an incurable romantic. He wondered about the singers. (Kaufmann too exuded sensitivity and sensuality.)

When the duet ended, Youtube provided a trio – Anna Netrebko, Placido Domingo, Rolando Villazon – singing an aria from *La Traviata* at an outdoor event in Brindisi. It was wonderful. But the old man noticed how Domingo had aged considerably and he asked himself how much longer the tenor's star would shine.

That morning the old man thought about all the stupendous music that had been created by human beings – the brilliant composers, musicians, and singers – and how music definitely was one of the greatest wonders of life before death.

THE OLD MAN AND THE DEFINITION OF "ROMANTICISM"

July 26, 2020

THE WORD "ROMANTICISM" was used by many people. The old man was one of them. The word meant many different things to many different people. Millions of pages had been written about the subject. The old man decided he would write down what the word meant to him.

Normally, he was allergic to *"isms"* – communism, socialism, capitalism, fascism, determinism, libertarianism, idealism, materialism, dualism, empiricism, rationalism, racism, sexism, classicism, asceticism, hedonism, nihilism, altruism… even romanticism. He hated trying to simplify the infinitely complex. That said, he still considered himself a "romantic".

Here's what the word *romantic* meant to the old man…

Life is an absolute mystery. Nobody has any idea how anything got be what it is. The mind is a mystery. The body is a mystery. Consciousness is a mystery. The galaxies are a mystery. The sun is a mystery. The earth is a mystery. Every creature thereupon is a mystery. Every cell, molecule, atom, and quark is a mystery. History has no beginning and no end. Every moment is infinitely complex… In the middle of all this is you, her, him, it, them and me. All of us are also unfathomable mysteries. The old man felt this every day. He had sensed it for decades. He had been on the brink of madness many times. What saved him? Moments of the deepest romance. Moments when he felt the most profound love for another creature. It could be a flower, a child, a piece of music, or a woman. He felt the greatest romance when in love with a woman. Hence, it was at such moments when folly was kept farthest at bay. Romance is what saved the old man from utter insanity.

That's what romanticism meant to him. That's how he defined it. He didn't care how anyone else defined it. He was respectful of their definitions. But he had his own truth. There wasn't any. Except love. Maybe.

THE OLD MAN AND THE BREADCRUMBS

July 27, 2020

THE OLD MAN had written millions of words, more than thirty books. As he thought about all these, the words and books, a simile came to mind: *Writing was like throwing breadcrumbs to birds, most of which are not very hungry.*

When the old man was younger and working as a teacher, he had often spent his lunch break sitting on a park bench eating a sandwich in a lovely park near the lake in Lausanne Ouchy. Inevitably, a flock of friends would wind up at his feet. He would always give them something and they always seemed hungry.

First, one or two would glide down from a tree and land a meter or two from his shoes. They would wait patiently. The younger version of the old man would eat most of his meal (but always saving a substantial chunk of bread for his friends) before tossing the first crumb or two. The "sparrows" (for that is what the world called these friends) would swiftly pounce-bounce and gobble them up in a New York minute. Friends of the friends, all seemingly very hungry, would then descend in rapid fire from surrounding trees. The younger old man would then break the remaining bread into Lilliputian pieces and distribute it until there was no more. He sometimes felt like Jesus.

Writing was different. His words were not fought for or awaited with urgency. If a few friends descended from their roosts and nibbled he was lucky. Rare were the people who tossed breadcrumbs from park benches in Ouchy. The birds seemed deeply appreciative when such a person appeared. Not so with the words the old man tossed to the world. There were writers everywhere and most readers were overfed. Unlike the breadcrumbs, the old man's words usually lay scattered on the ground uneaten.

Sometimes he thought he should have been a baker.

THE OLD MAN
AND LIVING AND DYING

July 28, 2020

THE OLD MAN had had many thoughts about living and dying. He remembered that as a younger old man the "Spaghetti Westerns" of Sergio Leone (with the help of Ennio Morricone's music) had provided moments of acute reflection about both subjects. What did it mean to be dead or alive? What controlled what? Was there an overlap? Could either be understood or defined? What was knowable and what was veiled? ... In any case, after years of rumination, the old man thought the word death was a misnomer and that we should stop saying this or that "died", but rather that it was *"returned to the infinite,"* e.g. *"Mother didn't die; she was returned to the infinite."* He thought that would be closer to the truth. For what was living if it was not giving the infinite a sense of finitude? Mother wasn't "dead; she had simply returned to where she came from – from "infinity", the home of all being forever and ever... For didn't we all float down the river of life and eventually get washed out into the great sea of eternal mystery? If there were no opposites in the universe – no up or down, high or low, big or small, beginning and end, hot or cold, then wasn't the same true for "life" and "death"?

And then the old man thought that if we could talk to all the billions and billions and billions of creatures that had already died, we would probably find out that dying wasn't such a big deal after all. Most likely, one falls asleep and has nothing to remember when one doesn't wake up...

THE OLD MAN AND THE END OF THE WORLD

July 28, 2020

THE OLD MAN did not believe in the end of the world. He didn't believe in the beginning of the world. Why not? … Why?

THE OLD MAN
AND HIS DAUGHTER'S TUITION

July 28, 2020

THE OLD MAN'S second daughter was about to start the university in Lausanne. She had chosen the field of psychology. The old man was happy for her and happy that university study in Switzerland was not absurdly expensive like it was across the ocean in America. Yesterday the bill came for her enrollment fee. It was 580. – CHF, or roughly $600.

Of course the old man thought he would quickly pay the bill and get it out of the way. Then he thought again: *Jodie has a couple of thousand francs saved in the bank. Why shouldn't she pay the bill? Wouldn't this make her appreciate her education more? Wouldn't she take it more seriously if it was "her" money, some of it hard earned? Are parents who "pay" for everything doing a disservice to their children?*

The old man had been the middle child of a family of five kids. He had watched his parents struggle to put the first two through college. He decided he would take no more money from his parents after age seventeen. He found a summer job after high school working in a greasy spoon in the Oakland ghetto. The pay was $3.20 an hour, which was quite good in 1967. He worked 40 to 60 hours a week, often doing extra shifts when guys called in sick. Every dollar counted. He did the job for four months every summer and when he was home for the Xmas holiday, often on Christmas Day and New Year's. *Doggie Diner* never closed, and he never had a vacation during his four university years. How could he take one? He needed the money for school.

The old man had long thought that working his way through school was perhaps more of an education than school itself. He had seen the "real world". He saw how people struggled. He saw how there were wonderful people of all sorts and kinds and all walks of life. He saw how important his education was. He saw how fortunate he was to come from a loving family and a nice neighborhood.

The old man wondered whether or not he should talk to his daughter and her mother about who should pay the $600 bill. Would they think him a tight wad? Would they understand that for him it wasn't about the money, but was only about what was best for his daughter?

What was best? This had been his thought and concern every moment throughout the lives of his three children. No one would ever know if he was ever right.

THE OLD MAN
AND THE PRACTICAL TASK

July 28, 2020

THE OLD MAN and his daughter were going to paint an outside railing that day, the one that goes up the steps to the front door. He had already sanded it. He thought preparing it was possibly a tougher job that the painting itself. He had used the electric sander and it had been a hot day and he had had to do many of the corners by hand.

The old man had a secret love affair with practical tasks like painting a railing. It allowed him moments where he could hide from the infinite complexity of the world. He would thoroughly immerse himself in the activity and would forget about everything else.

The old man was not much of a handyman, but when he put his mind in it, he usually got pretty good results. In a way, he envied people who submerged themselves in jobs, religions, causes, and practical tasks. They were magicians who turned the infinite into the finite. They were able to do more than give life meaning, direction, and purpose; they were able to melt into that meaning, direction, and purpose and become one with it. Instead of standing alone on top of an icy mountain peak or trekking in solitary through Death Valley or drifting aimlessly on a raft in the middle of the ocean, they were able to conjoin with *"the world"*. They were able to merge with something… anything… and escape the loneness of desolation.

The old man did not seek solitude. It was not a goal. He did not see it as a sign of superiority or prestige. It was simply where his mind took him. He saw infinity in every moment, every creature, every *thing*. He had not chosen his path any more than birds choose to have wings. He knew he would enjoy painting the railing with his daughter. Lucky are those who unite in task and, even more so, with someone they love.

THE ... MAN AND THE ... DAY

July 30, 2020

ONCE UPON A time there was a man and a day. Was the man old or young? Who could ever say? One never knew how much living was left. Was the day beautiful or ugly? One could never know until the day was done.

The man looked at the day. It was there, before him. He would live it. We are all condemned to live every day until we die. *How much life can be squeezed out of a day? Perhaps a better question is: How much life can be squeezed INTO a day?* The man thought, *We must make the day; the day must not make us.*

The man looked at the day and said, "I will make you. You won't make me."

And the day whispered, *"Ah... en fin..."*

THE OLD MAN AND THE SWISS NATIONAL HOLIDAY

August 1, 2020

WHEN ONE SUCCESSFULLY migrates one finds a new home. Strange things become familiar. Foreign license plates cease to be foreign. The air and land and language become normal.

Everyone has a home, the old man thought. Some of us have multiple homes. Unbeknownst to most of us, we all share a home. It is round like a basketball and flies through space unending unstopping.

Today is the Swiss National Holiday. Red and white flags come out of the cupboards and closets. Switzerland and the old man adopted each other and both adapted as well.

But he knew that there were people out there who had left their homes and had difficulty finding a new one. These people were called "refugees".

The old man scratched his head and thought that if all people one day finally understood that the little earth was *home* for everybody, then national holidays would not necessarily cease to exist, but would at least take on a subtler meaning.

THE OLD MAN
AND THE PRESIDENT AND GUNS

August 2, 2020

PEOPLE SHOULD STOP bitching about the president. They should instead bitch about the way their country selects the president. How can anyone blame Mr. Trump for wanting to be president of the mightiest nation? How can anyone blame Mr. Biden for wanting to fulfill his lifelong dream, even at an age when he is far past his prime? Mr. Biden and Mr. Trump are the problem before our eyes. But the real problem is a system that puts two men like this in the ring for the Heavyweight Championship bout. It is like instead of having Mohammed Ali and Sonny Liston duking it out in the "Thrilla in Manilla", the public is supposed to watch Groucho Marx fighting Jerry Lewis – great comedians, but boxers not.

The old man thought that neither Mr. Trump nor Mr. Biden had any real business living in the White House. Few, if any, presidents in the last fifty years have had any business sitting on America's throne. The elections are a media circus wherein everybody is throwing punches below the belt and most of the people who judge the winners – the voters – are highly uninformed as to what is going on in the world or the country. The whole thing is a joke, but we the people cannot step back and get a perspective on the idiocy, lunacy, folly, and foolishness of what's going on. Were the Founding Fathers alive today, they would surely rewrite much of the Constitution, especially the way the president is selected.

The old man lives in Switzerland. He has something with which to compare the American system. Both countries are democracies, but in the old man's opinion, Switzerland is a far better democracy. An example of its superiority is how the Swiss select their president. There is no campaigning. There is a multi-party system. (The two-party system is as archaic as God vs. Satan.) The Executive Branch is composed of seven people who are elected by the Congress, i.e. by people who generally have years and years of experience and a reasonable sense of "what's going on". Each member of the "Federal Council" serves as president for one year. There is no silly primary system and campaign fiasco with candidates spending millions of francs and babbling absurd rallying cries on television and in front of roaring crowds wearing sloganized hats and t-shirts. Solid qualified people get elected to run the country, not one mega-mediatized darling of the moment.

Trump and Biden are the immediate problem in America. But Trump and Biden are not the real problem. The real problem is much deeper, lost in the depths of the constitution and wholly warped by the changes that have occurred in the world since 1776, i.e. the way the President of the United States is selected. No one is to blame, but a metamorphosis is badly needed.

The same is true for guns in America. But the change for them should be far harsher. They should cease to exist. Were the old man the president, he would ban them all.

THE OLD MAN
AND CHRISTOPHE VARIDEL

August 4, 2020

THE OLD MAN spent thirty-five years of his life playing and coaching basketball in Switzerland. He had just finished writing a book called, *Of Hoops and Men... The Unofficial History of Swiss Basketball*, wherein he talked about all the amazing people and players he had the pleasure of knowing through the sport. However, the old man recently realized that he had failed to write a word about the most talented Swiss player ever to play the game. This was not really his fault because the old man had ended his career in 2013 (which was when the book ended), and it was precisely at that moment that the most talented Swiss player was exhibiting his skills across two oceans, and hence, very little information about him was floating back to Switzerland.

His name was Christophe Varidel. He was twenty-two years old, a student-athlete at Chaminade University in Hawaii. That season, in 2013, he played in a total of five games. He averaged 21 points per game while shooting 46% from behind the 3-point line. Against Baylor University (a perennial powerhouse in America) in a pre-season tournament, Christophe Varidel scored 42 points and made ten 3-pointers! These were otherworldly statistics, much like the great Stephan Curry had when he was at the university. No Swiss player had ever done such a thing at such a high level. Shortly after, Christophe seriously injured his knee and disappeared from the basketball radar screen.

The old man had never realized what an amazing basketball player Christophe Varidel was until last week, when he came to the old man's house for lunch. Varidel had written a book and asked the old man if he would read it and give him suggestions. The book was to help young players develop their basketball skills. In it, Varidel explained what he went through in order to have a chance to play at such a high level. He called it "The Varidel Method". Rarely had the old man seen someone so dedicated to a task and a dream. Varidel had spent thousands and thousands of hours alone in a gym – often with the lights turned off so he wouldn't be discovered – developing his basketball skills. He became a great player, but few people in his home country knew about him.

The moral of the story is that there are so many wonderful human beings out there that we know little or nothing about. We are so in the dark about so much. With a few strokes of luck the old man was convinced that a Swiss basketball player named Christophe Varidel could have become a veritable star in the basketball universe. It didn't happen because of a knee injury. But seven years later he had written a rough draft of a book to help upcoming young players realize their basketball dreams.

The old man strongly encouraged Varidel to finish and publish the book. He even suggested that Varidel consider re-uniting with his own basketball dream. He was only twenty-nine and, for the first time in years, his knee was fully operational again. Varidel said he now had other interests like playing the piano, dancing, reading, writing, and learning about the world (he talked a little about women too), and that he wasn't sure if he wanted to devote so much time to basketball again. The old man fully understood.

Later, the old man watched the *YouTube* highlights of his 42-point game vs. Baylor. It was something to behold.

THE OLD MAN AND LOVELESS LIVING

August 6, 2020

THE OLD MAN spent the night dreaming about trying to make sure that all 400 kids, coaches, and staff were having a good time in camp. He woke up realizing that camp had been cancelled and how he was sick of loveless living.

The camp had gone on for forty straight years. The old man started it in 1980 to try to use the game of basketball to make people happy. That's all he ever tried to do as camp director: make people happy and try to help them appreciate life and respect other creatures. Simple formula. Of course he wanted to help the campers become better basketball players, too. But it could have been dancing or ping-pong.

But now it was 2020, the "Year of the Corona", and the camp had been cancelled. The dreams hadn't. He really did dream that he was in camp and his mind kept harping on the dozens of details that had to be taken care of the next day. And when he woke up, he really was haunted by the thought of how loveless living was wearing him down.

What did he mean by "loveless living"? It was simple, and he wondered how many millions of people in the world shared his situation, i.e. spent years and years – even decades… even life… – not sharing body and mind with someone they loved passionately or even a bit less. The old man appreciated solitude, but there were limits. Without love, solitude eventually became a cumbersome affair.

The old man thought of his cat. It could go for a day or two without coming to him to be stroked. But eventually it always came back, circled his feet, and demanded (and got) a long series of caresses, which always ended in a string of purrs. Tilou knew what he needed and wanted. The old man knew what he needed and wanted. Tilou was by far the more successful of the two.

When the old man thought about why he had lived lovelessly for such long stretches of his life, he could always come up with a series of semi-rational explanations, e.g. he knew he was overly sensitive and put far more emphasis on the sensual side of life than most creatures; he loved the flesh, and like Matisse, he was obsessively enchanted by the female form; he found few people with whom he could converse about "life" and its infinite complexity and mystery; as he aged, fewer and fewer people wanted to sample his flesh, and he too became pickier about whose flesh he wanted to share; the woman he lived with long ago decided their relationship had been amputated of all *love-like* sharing; most people were already up to their ears in complicated relationships and hence very few were free to plunge into anything new, etc., etc., etc.

And so life wore on and the old man wondered if he would ever live love again. Unfortunately, the cat never reciprocated during the petting sessions, but then again, he and Tilou never did have much to talk about.

THE OLD MAN AND THE UNGRATEFUL BASTARDS

August 7, 2020

THE OLD MAN had been a boy in sunny California, thriving like thistle in a garden of post-war optimism. The Beaver was always happy at the end of the show, Donna Reed was the perfect mother, and Father inevitably knew what was best. The streets were wide, the schools were new, the mowed lawn smelled like honey, and friends, teachers, parents, and Sam Stovall, the Little League coach, loved the young man. America was beautiful. Cars were comfortable, girls were cute, and God was caring for everybody.

Then things changed. Two Kennedys and two Kings got killed. Vietnam became a horror show. Watts rioted. Africa starved. AIDS humbled science. The world lost its luster. The old man went to the university and lost his faith in god, truth, teleology, and morality. The Garden of Eden was full of weeds. The young old man decided he needed a change of air. He left America and moved to Switzerland.

There, on the shores of Lake Geneva, he found a new sort of paradise. Unemployment was near zero, no one locked a door, streets and sidewalks were spotless, mountains and vineyards were glorious, and he was surrounded by lots of contented hard-working people. The world became a positive place again. God hadn't made a return, but people were doing a decent job of running the show. The middle-aged old man was happy working, playing, and raising a family.

Then, as the twentieth century melted into the twenty-first, the not-yet old man felt a change coming on. Cell phones, CNN, the Internet, and hundreds of TV channels. Suddenly the constant consternations of the world were thrown into everyone's face. All day of every day people everywhere were being made aware of what was wrong with the world. Their minds were bombarded with the negative. The problems of the world had become omnipresent. Slowly but surely, the citizens of the world were becoming entrenched in a kind of global pessimism. God's death had been bad enough for our tender noggins. But now every hardship, calamity, misfortune, and woe became the focus of our attention. The bombardment of negativity was non-stop. The news prospered. And of course for news people, the bigger the catastrophe the higher the ratings. The old man noticed that everywhere he went, human beings had begun to see life through glasses of gloom and doom.

He thought this was tragic. He pondered: *People today have completely lost sight of the fact that they are living in what is by far the most wonderful time on planet earth. They have a million advantages and blessings that no other group of humans has ever had. And yet all they do is bitch about the world. They see the worst of everything everywhere. They forget all the good and beauty of the world. They forget how lucky they are. They have been blinded by the negativity of the news. They have lost sight of everything that is "right" about the world and are obsessed with what is "wrong"... And they are also oblivious to the fact that the world has never been "a nice place". There has always been a huge amount of suffering. The world has always been a gargantuan slaughterhouse. All creatures – from dinosaurs to insects – must eat to live. Death is everywhere. All creatures are killers. Under every step any of us take there is the dust of the dead. In 1800, the average life expectancy was 34 years of age in Europe and 26 in Africa. The*

Spanish Plague of 1918 killed an estimated 50,000,000 people. World War II saw 70,000,000 die, and no one bothered to count the animals. But today we do count them and 150,000,000 are killed every day for human consumption. (Imagine how many animals are killed for "animal" consumption every moment of every day!) ... Yes, the world has always been a horror show... But... But... But today we are living in what is by far the most wonderful time on planet earth. We have our incredible supermarkets, schools, hospitals, clothes, cars, airplanes, heaters, air-conditioners, restaurants, etc. And yet nobody seems to notice. Everybody is too busy bitching to appreciate anything. They all bitch about Trump, Biden, the police, covid, inequality, global warming, sexual harassment... Bitch, bitch, bitch. Negativity all day and all night. People seeing the worst of everything and forgetting all the good and beauty of the world. Forgetting everything that is "right" with the world and obsessing with what is "wrong". Like spoiled rich unappreciative children who have no perspective on anything and only complain about what they "don't" have.

Of course... the old man thought in response to people murmuring and bitching at him for being "insensitive"... *of course we want to heal poverty and injustice and strive to make the world a better place. But as we do so we should never lose sight of what an amazing place it already is and the incredible good fortune we have of being part of the living... today!*

Really, are there many things worse than a room full of ungrateful bastards?

THE OLD MAN AND HIS FAVOURITE SHOES (AND THE WEASEL)

August 11, 2020

HE HAD AT least twelve pairs of shoes, the old man did. Oh, maybe more. No one was counting, especially not the old man.

Three or four pairs were lying on the carpet in the bedroom near his bed. The others were next to or under his ancient armoire. The armoire had followed him through Switzerland for more than forty years. He bought it at the Salvation Army in Lausanne for 400 francs, which was a good sum of money for someone who was making a bit over 2,000 a month. Originally, it was big enough for all his clothes.

The armoire had to be one of the few such pieces of furniture in Europe with a bullet hole through the back. It was on the left side where shelves house his pullovers, shorts, and jeans. The right side was for hanging things. The bullet had flown from the rifle of a forest ranger and had transpierced the forehead of a weasel before hitting the back of the armoire.

The old man always thought the story was worth telling because it represented, as well as anything, how crazily arbitrary life and death were. Was "arbitrary" the right word? Maybe contingent, designless, fortuitous, accidental, adventitious, capricious, haphazard, random, blind, unpredictable, fickle, flighty, birdbrained, frivolous, dizzying, irrational, indiscriminate, chaotic, jumbled, unsystematic, slipshod, senseless, illogical, bananas, bonkers, strange, uncanny, or absurd might be closer to the point… though the point itself was not clear. And then again, maybe deterministic, inevitable, and necessary should be added to the list. Or perhaps words like incredible, wondrous, glorious, mind-blowing, stupendous, and even "divine" came closest to describing what existence really was.

In any case, the death of the weasel had depended on a few billion other things happening, among them was the old man's marriage to his ex-wife and their brief rental of the ground floor of a house in Grandvaux. All that would not have come to pass had he not met her one quiet lonely Sunday night in a bar near the cathedral in Lausanne at the precise moment he had suddenly felt that he had had enough frolicking as a free bachelor. It could also be noted that the weasel would have had a longer life had the newlyweds not taken a weekend vacation to Mürren in the Jungfrau region and had not had a cat that had recently hatched kittens, and hence, when husband and wife went away one Friday morning in 1983, they left a window open so the cats could go in and out of the house which was located near some vineyards and a small forest.

It turns out that the ex-wife had had a jealousy crisis during the weekend (this had no effect on the weasel's longevity, but did influence the number of years the couple stayed together) and asked the young old man to deposit her at her mother's house when they came back from Mürren. The mother had graciously offered to take care of their one-year-old son while they went to the mountains. So the young old man dropped his even younger wife off at her mom's place and went home to Grandvaux alone.

When he walked into the house it was an absolute mess.

Lamps were knocked off tables; there was excrement on the telephone; a box of dried baby milk was open on the living room floor; the cupboards in the kitchen were open; cereal boxes and a packet of flour had been ripped open; some other lumps of shit were stuck on the stove...

The young old man looked at the chaos and simply imagined the cats had had a grand party. He began cleaning up. Eventually he went into the bedroom. There, he immediately noticed that some of his sweaters were scattered on the floor at the foot of the armoire. He bent down and picked one up. As he rose to put it on a shelf, a calm beatific triangular head appeared from behind a fluffy pullover. The young old man jumped back, scurried out the door and shut it carefully.

The fact that it was a Sunday might have also been a factor in the weasel's lifespan. When the woman who answered the phone at the Société pour la Protection des Animaux asked the young old man exactly what kind of animal was in his armoire, he said "Madame, I have no idea what kind of creature it is. If I knew, I might not be calling you!" The woman said she was sorry, but that if he couldn't identify the animal, she couldn't do anything for him...

So the young old man called the police down in the road in Cully. This time the voice on the other end whistled a different tune. When he told the policeman that the animal had looked very calm and serene, the officer said it was probably a weasel and it probably had rabies. He said there had been cases in the area recently and that a rabid animal always went through a period of calm before it lost its mind and started attacking. When the young old man told the policeman he had cleaned up the mess in the living room and kitchen before seeing the animal in the bedroom, the officer said that he (the young old man) now was most certainly contaminated and that he would need to be quarantined. Then the officer said, "We'll be there as soon as possible."

"We" was a policeman and a forest ranger. Before entering the bedroom, the cop drew his pistol and the forest ranger cocked his rifle. They stealthily entered the room while the young old man stood at the door. He pointed to the shelf at eye level inside the open armoire. The ranger's head suddenly jerked back an inch or two. His eyes froze. "If that weasel doesn't have rabies," he whispered, "I'm the Pope." He slowly raised his rifle and fired.

The old man never forgot what happened next. The animal jumped from the armoire, flew under the bed, shit, and died.

The men put on plastic gloves and packed the weasel in a transparent bag. It would be sent to Bern for analysis. The young old man would stay quarantined in the house until they had the results.

Four days later the phone finally rang. The young old man was freed and out of danger. The weasel had been as healthy as the cats that eventually came back. The weasel had had a house to itself for three days and a soft bed in the armoire.

The young old man and the ex-wife lived sixteen more interesting years together.

So what about the old man's favorite shoes? They're the ones that he bought in Portugal seven years ago. They were very cheap, something like 29 euros. He got them in a small store on the main street in Qaurteira, the small town next to the chic community of Villamoura where they were staying on holiday. He, his girlfriend, and their eleven-year-old daughter had walked there along the beach to see how the other half lived. A pleasant elderly man ran the store alone. He told the old man that though the shoes were very inexpensive, they were of excellent quality. The old man bought the shoes as a souvenir and because of the kindness of the shoe man. He didn't really need a new pair of loafers.

There were at least six pairs of loafer-type shoes under the armoire. One pair cost over 400 Swiss francs (thirteen times more than his favorites). The others were all around a hundred dollars, francs or euros. But none was as comfortable as the ones he had bought in the little shoe store in Portugal with his new family before he became an old man. The past seven years he has worn them more than any others. He never has to bend down to slip them on. On his feet they feel like an extra layer of soft warm skin. They are light beige-brown. When he bought them he didn't really like the color that much. All his other shoes were darker. But now these were his favorites by a long shot.

Speaking of shots, the old man imagined that until his dying day, he would remember the shoes as much as the innocent weasel that got the bullet through the head.

The weasel went "pop". Do shoes have *souls?*

THE OLD MAN
AND THE HULY BUBLE

A day in June, 2010

ONCE UPON A time, a time when things were happening just like they are now, but with variations of course, Gud decided that there was too much seriousness in the behavior of trees, rocks, spinning planets, and sunsets, so Hu decided to create mun and wumun. At first there was just one mun and one wumun, but Gud, being one to plan ahead, gave the mun a punus and the wumun a vuguna and the next thing Hu knew there were mun and wumun of different colors and sizes all over the place. In the beginning Gud really liked watching them fight over things like big sticks and pieces of meat, and Hu often laughed his uss off. All of this lasted for quite a long while and Gud stayed reasonably amused... But, as always, boredom began to set in and Hu decided to make a few changes. First Hu decided to make the mun and wumun talk, you know, make noises with their muuths and tongues and lips. But after a while these noises got to be very repetitive and Gud got bored again, so he decided to put a bruun in the heads of all the mun and wumun. Up until this point all the decisions that the mun and wumun made were made in their punuses and vugunas and muuths. But now, with a bruun in their heads, they had another engine to tell them what to do and which way to go.

It's funny how all the mun and wumun started to take their

bruuns seriously. Whereas before, when the punuses and vugunas and muuths were responsible for what was going on, suddenly there were a whole bunch of new things happening in Gud's funhouse. And the biggest things were all of the sudden the establishment of rulugions and murulities. Suddenly mun and wumun – mostly mun actually – started inventing all kinds of guds and murul principles telling everybody what was rught and what was wrung. Up until then everybody was just kind of eating, sleeping, furnicating, and dying, but suddenly people started writing books and giving speeches and seeing anguls and having vusions about guds and stuff like that, and climbing up mountains and telling everybody what was rught and wrung and how to luve their luves.

In Chuna there were people like Cunfucius. He was probably a pretty nice guy who didn't overeat.

In Jupon there were things like "The Seven Guds of Guud Luck".

In Undia there were the Hundus with Guds all over the place running around with hules in their shoes.

And thun thure was the Bug Duddy Buddhu who got his picture in lots of buuks and his stutue in gurduns and who liked dusserts and second helpings of fuud.

In Muxico the sun was Gud for a while until the Chrustians came.

In the Muddle East there was the muuntain-climber named Muses who had a gud that got mad a lot and threw lightening bults at sunners.

The Gruuks had some prutty guud guds too who even liked to drink guud wine and shuw off their punuses and vugunas.

Then came Jusus who was really probably a prutty nice guy, but who got killed and accused of things like wulking on water and feeding fuve thousand people with twulve luuves of bread by people like Puul, Juhn, Luuk, and Muthuw who started wruting the Huly Buble.

Pretty suun there was a string of Pupes who got lots of muney, ate well, built nice buuldings for themsulves and started a series of wars.

Then Muhummud came long with Ullah and scarves became fashuunable along with cutting off hunds and fungers.

Then there were puuple like Luthur and Culvun who had seen enuugh of the Pupes and started new rulugions also based on thu Huly Buble.

Then came the Prutustunts and the Murmuns, and the Juhuvuhs Wutnussus and the Suvunth Duy Udvuntusts and the Buptusts, all kinds of gruups like that that were telling puuple what was rught and wrung and whu the real Gud wus.

It really got to be a big muss and the real Gud wus becuming less and less amused by the whule shuw. Hu started thunking maybe Hu shuuldn't have put that bruun in the mun's and wumun's heads after all.

Hu finully ducided to have a big fluud and into the gurbage can went most of the muss.

THE OLD MAN AND THE CRABS ON THE BOTTOM OF THE OCEAN

August 13, 2020

THERE REALLY WERE crabs on the bottom of the ocean. They were born there, they lived there, they died there. Millions, maybe billions of them. Scholars said there were approximately 3,500,000,000,000 sea-dwelling animals. Hmmm… A lot was going on in that water…

The old man tried to imagine what it would like to be a crab. He tried to think of similarities that men might have with crabs. There was one glaring parallel: no crab had asked to be a crab; no man had asked to be a man. Then there was the human skull and the protective shell on the crab. That was an interesting similarity. The old man wondered why some creatures were more protected than others. People liked to think crabs and snails had shells *for a reason*, i.e. for protection. The old man thought this was nonsense. If snails had shells to protect themselves, why didn't slugs have shells? Why didn't butterflies have shells? Or chickens that got eaten by foxes all the time?... Because crabs had shells maybe *they* are able to protect themselves from many predators. But that was not *"why"* they had shells. Humans didn't have fingers so they could put socks on, play the piano, and build atomic bombs. They put on socks, played the piano, and built atom bombs

BECAUSE they had fingers (and brains and eyes, etc).

The old man thought that as long as humans thought things existed and happened *for a reason*, they would continue to see the world falsely and naively – something we as a race have done for millennia.

In the future, the old man thought, the enlightened man would understand that nothing in existence existed for a reason. Everything simply existed and then things happened based on what existed. Armadillos didn't have shells *in order to* protect themselves; armadillos *were able to* protect themselves *because* they had shells. Snakes weren't legless *so* they could slither; they slithered *because* they had no legs. Petrol didn't exist *so* we could burn it for energy; we burned it for energy *because* it existed. Crabs didn't exist *so* we could eat them; we ate them *because* they existed and our taste buds liked them. Crabs weren't wingless and finless *so* they could crawl on the ocean floor; they crawled on the ocean floor *because* they were finless and wingless. The sun didn't exist so we could stay warm and plants could grow. We stayed warm and plants grew because the sun existed… This was how the universe worked. Not the other way around. Humans were not created in order to build skyscrapers, cars, computers, casinos, iPhones, and televisions. All these things came into existence because they were simply part of what humans did. But there was no glorious plan or logic behind, crabs, slugs, skyscrapers, TVs, or anything else.

The old man pondered. And the more he thought about the world, the more he thought humans tended to have things sideways.

THE OLD MAN AND THE HERD

August 18, 2020

THE OLD MAN reflected on the "herd" ("le troupeau" in French). For many, the word had a negative connotation. This was not the case for the old man. It was simply a way of describing a huge amount of human behavior, i.e. people moving about, thinking, and acting in herds. This was what went through the old man's mind:

That many other "animals" stay together in herds says nothing pejorative about them. I would never presume that the life of a solitary fox is in any way superior to the life of a goose that always flies in a flock or a fish that swims in a school. Each creature is simply doing what it does in the way it does it. I have said many times that calling a human an animal does not denigrate the two-legged creature, but rather flatters him or her. Both human and animal are wonderful creatures, miraculous creatures. I recently heard a renowned fly specialist say that 70% of the DNA of Homo Sapiens and Diptera (flies) is exactly the same. That any of us exists at all is the greatest wonder and mystery of all. In any case, many creatures on earth have a strong predilection (call it "instinct" if you prefer…) for being part of a herd.

Goats, sheep, fish, cows, birds, camels, horses, ants, humans, and many other creatures often stick together for a myriad of reasons. But the human type interests me most of all. – Do not most men and women have a powerful need to be part of a herd? Do we not get our identity from the herd? Do we not constantly seek approbation for "who we are" and "what we believe" by mixing with people who share our vision of the world? It seems very apparent that the human mantra is, "Give me someone to follow... and quick!"

But this is not a bad thing... it is a human thing. However, most "intellectuals" (I use the word loosely of course) have a rather tenacious tendency to belittle the herd. When they say that we are herd animals they mean it to reflect badly or negatively on our poor battered species. My inverted reasoning sees absolutely nothing wrong with the herd and wishes to point out that 99% of the intellectuals who browbeat "the masses" (perhaps in an attempt to feel superior to them) do exactly the same thing (i.e. behave herd-like) in that they too are inevitably looking for friends who agree with them, and are usually trying to recruit followers of their own. They are simply part of the anti-herd herd...

By pointing this out, I do not want to attack our dear intellectuals, but rather make them think about their thinking. I want everybody to think about his or her thinking. I want everyone to understand that we are all part of the great innocence of existence. None of us are above or below it. We are all part of the soup. No creature asked to be born with the brain and body it has. We are all innocent. All being is innocent. By declaring this I wish to cleanse the world of all its guilt and sin. I want everyone to understand that there is nothing wrong with being a herd human. If you are one, you should accept it and live your life happily in your "herdiness". Don't be ashamed of being a "herd" human. Admit what you are and try to have a certain feeling of pride... but not a pride wherein you try to elevate yourself "above" other creatures. You are not above; you are next to. There is no above and below in the universe. It seems that only we in our silliness create such stratifications. If you are a lone wolf or a solitary eagle, of course you too should try to enjoy your lot, enjoy being what you are. But do not belittle the apples on the tree, the bees in the hive, the men and women huddled in the church; do not look "down" on the rest of the world. You don't criticize the sun for being the sun or the moon for being the moon; by the same token you shouldn't criticize an ant for being an ant or a herd human for being a herd human. I have said it a thousand times: Nothing can be other that what it is. When the world *understands this it will have a chance to have a certain peace. When the world understands this it will take a giant step toward washing away the piles of sin, guilt, blame, and hate that has heretofore sullied Eden.*

Thinkers of the world unite! Let the herds be! Realize that we are all wallowing in the pen… together!

Thus thought the old man one spring day.

THE OLD MAN AND TOILET PAPER AND THINGS

August 20, 2020

SUDDENLY – AS SUDDENLY as bats appear in an evening sky – the old man had a thought: *I don't think I've ever heard a mention of "toilet paper" in all of literature. The moment has come to right the wrong.* And the old man chuckled.

With time he had come to appreciate many of the simple things in life. *What,* he thought, *could be simpler than toilet paper? Was there anything more universal than cleaning one's tush? Excepting the very young and the very old, everybody does it every day of life. In a subtle slippery way, it might be claimed that toilet paper was the one thing that united the whole human family.*

There were two new discount supermarkets that were spreading across the globe almost as quickly as the coronavirus… Aldi and Lidl. They had a different way of doing things. They cut out all the unnecessary parts of shopping for food and so-called "household necessities". They had their top quality-price standard products. But as for the other stuff – stuff like clothes, tools, foreign beer, kids toys, special sauces and such, every time you went into the store there was a new selection. And sometimes prices were so low they boggled eyes and minds.

The old man noticed that Lidl and Aldi had the best toilet paper he had ever used. He couldn't decide whose was better. Both were sturdy and soft, and each piece was long enough to be folded and used alone. With the 4-layer version you never needed to double up with two pieces and no matter how hard the fingers pushed the paper never broke. What more could one ask for in *papier de toilette?*

Imagine where we would be without toilet paper. We've all tried leaves or newspaper in moments of desperation. And o my goodness, how those occasions made us appreciate good tender paper!

The old man ruminated thus: *Isn't the appreciation of all things appreciable one of the keys to a happy life and world?*

THE OLD MAN AND BEING WRONG

August 23, 2020

THE OLD MAN delighted in being wrong. There was nothing wrong with being wrong, except refusing to admit it when it was obviously the case. If we want right in the world, we should be delighted to know when we are wrong such that we can add to the right. Like most people, the old man liked to see wrongs righted, including his own. Recognizing that one could be wrong was certainly a sign of being the *right* kind of person.

Yesterday the old man found out he had been wrong about toilet paper. He thanked a friend (a world traveler) for correcting him. The friend explained that not everybody in the world used toilet paper. It seems that the Japanese have very sophisticated ways of cleaning their keesters. They have special toilets with shoots of soap and water (and a warm-air drying system) that do the trick in a very agreeable manner with no paper or wiping. The old man was so happy to hear this – and so happy to be wrong – that had it not been for the coronavirus voyage restrictions, he might have jumped on the Internet and bought himself a ticket to Tokyo…

The friend went on to say that in countries where people follow the teachings of the prophet Muhammad there were also different ways of dealing with posterior hygiene, cleaning that involved hoses and tubes. This surprised the old man because he had been to Morocco and Tunisia and had not encountered anything but toilet paper. But the friend said that this was because the old man had been in touristy places. Again, the old man was happy to be corrected for his error and mistaken view of the world.

The old man knew that it was the nature of the brain to think it was right. Having observed the world for many decades, he had noticed that people rarely changed their minds about what they thought was true and false and good and bad. In some ways this was a sad commentary on the human species. But in other ways it was a positive thing because it allowed people to protect themselves from too much complexity and cognitive dissonance. If minds were better off with simplistic beliefs, wasn't it right to allow them such?

It occurred to the old man that perhaps the rightest brains were the ones that were prepared to admit they were wrong about almost everything, and that they would also be wrong to hope that humans would suddenly massively migrate to territories where the dominate climate was one of doubt and openness to the wonder of existence.

THE OLD MAN AND THE INFINITE

August 24, 2020

THE OLD MAN sensed he was close to the finish line. Not death, but having nothing else to say. He had written so much. He had come to the point where he felt infinity in every moment of anything and everything. Perhaps the last lines of his last book would be: *The history of everything is infinite. Yes, every smidgen of existence is infinitely complex and beyond comprehension. Blessings to all.*

But seemingly he was not quite there yet.

THE OLD MAN AND THE FINAL QUESTION

August 25, 2020

SLEEP HAD MANY faces for the old man. Sometimes it was choppy like a stormy sea. Sometimes it was as peaceful as a mountain lake on a silent spring morning. When sleep ended and a new day began, the old man often lay in the dark and his mind began to offer suggestions as to what he would write that morning. It was usually around five and before his corner of the earth had turned toward the sun.

This morning the mind began to wonder how many different ways a human being could die. The possibilities were endless: at birth, choking, mumps, measles, malaria, car accident, plane crash, an errant bullet or brick, poisoning, polio, drowning, heart failure, kidney failure, cancer, stroke, fire, drug overdose, an error on an operating table, leukemia, exhaustion, starvation, dehydration, suicide, murder, abortion, old age, etc. The potential ways one might cease to live were seemingly limitless.

Then the old man wondered if the possibilities for living were equally vast. Did a human being have infinite ways of living his or her life?

At first glance, the old man thought, *there are a million ways one can live and a million ways one can die… But is this really true? There will only be one death for each of us. And it will happen at one moment and in one way. Is the same not true for life, i.e. that string of moments that we call "our lives"? Every moment is lived in one way... the way it is lived in that moment. Hence, just like one cannot go back and die a different death, one can never go back and live a different life. Hence, every moment of life is really like the moment of death... It will only happen once, and it will happen the way it happens. Of course, life has "more moments" than death. But each of those moments is similarly immutable.*

Does this hold true for all existence?

This, the old man thought, *was the final question?*

THE OLD MAN AND THE DEATH OF RACE

August 31, 2020

THE OLD MAN thought about the world all the time. Here we are, flying through space on a huge ball of matter, millions of miles from an enormous sphere of fire that heats us and allows us to live and whose gravitational pull keeps us from flying off into deep space. Most of us are deader than doornails. None of us lives for a very long time. When the chips are down we really have no idea what existence is and how it came to be – if, in fact, "it came to be", for it is very possible that it has always existed and is simply constantly changing form. We are but a tiny dot in a quasi-infinite cosmos. And our so-called "civilization" is so infantile having started only a few thousand years ago, which is a blink of the eye for Being. We tend to lose sight of the mystery and wonder of all existence as we get so caught up in our "daily lives". We are such self-centered and self-absorbed creatures that have very little perspective on "the big picture", whatever it might be. The French use the word "nombriliste", meaning we have trouble seeing past our belly buttons.

And now, the old man wanted to make a point to the world about the world. He saw his point to be a follow up to his friend Nietzsche's point, i.e. "God is dead". Nietzsche and the old man both thought that as long as people believed in an afterlife, this life on earth would be degraded, cheapened, and devalued. However, if there was no god (and they saw no sign of one) and this existence was all any of us would have, then life on this earth would become infinitely more precious for everyone. Until mankind stopped believing in gods, bogus teleologies, other worlds, and spurious moralities, we humans would never feel and discover the glory of existence.

The old man's point was: "Race is dead". He thought that as long as men and women believed in "race", people would never see the truth about the glorious individuality and uniqueness of every creature on this earth, human or otherwise. With no god watching over the world, guiding the world, or judging the world, suddenly mankind had the huge responsibility of giving meaning to life. And by not grouping individuals into simplistic categories such as "race", or "nationality", or "species", all creatures could become unique and, who knew... even *divine*.

It seemed to the old man that God was still agonizing on the cross of the human mind. (It seemed quite clear that the so-called "animal" kingdom had lived quite well without *Him*.) *Race* was also an idea that still lingered in the minds of most people... – The old man once had a wonderful dog named "Finette". People used to ask him what "race" she was. He would always answer thus: "Finette had two parents, and those two parents had two parents, and those two parents had two parents, and those two parents had two parents and those two parents had two parents. That's already 64 dogs that went into making Finette, and we're only back to about 1950!" The interlocutor would inevitably give the old man a puzzled look and then say, "Yes... yes... but what *'race'* is she?"

For Finette to exist, millions – even billions or trillions – of "dogs" had to have existed. The same is true for humans. We all go back farther than we can imagine. There is no such thing as a pure race. Believing so is as simplistic as believing in God. Color does not a "race" make. Hair type does not a race make. Eye shape does not a race make. It is all naïve thinking. Culture is real; but race is not. And in today's world cultures constantly overlap. Each of us is an infinitely complex mix of chromosomes and cultures....

Thus the old man pondered. From a very early age the old man had looked around himself and had seen injustice, inequality, suffering and death. And he saw it everywhere. He knew it was rampant in the world and always had been. At the age of twenty he almost killed himself as he observed horrors like the Mai Lai massacre in Vietnam (a whole village of women, children, and old men slaughtered by crazed soldiers... war does that kind of thing to people), or when the neighbor up the street got murdered in his garage, or when the dog got hit by a car and lay dead on the street in a crimson pile of blood and fur, or when he went to Oakland and saw homeless people lying against walls and in gutters, or when his Aunt Betty tried to kill herself with a butcher knife, or when he saw animals viciously attacking and eating each other, or when he saw pictures of mothers and emaciated babies in Africa, or when he thought about the Native Americans having their land stolen, or films about slavery or gladiators in Rome. Even watching insects get massacred edged him toward insanity. Didn't they too have a right to live?!! – So at the university the young old man tried to help the poor and the mentally handicapped. He had a clothing drive and sent dozens of huge boxes full of garments to the NAACP in Mississippi. He tried to stop the war in Vietnam and the senseless killing of animals large and small. He saw problems everywhere, and the realization the earth was a very cruel place almost did him in.

Eventually the young old man decided that the world was far more complex than he had ever imagined and that he would either have to love it or leave it. He knew he could not change the world, and even if he could, there would still always be the eaters and the eaten. As he grew out of his youth, he decided he would simply always try to be kind, understanding, helpful, and courteous to every person and animal he came in contact with. This he could do. In fact, he thought this was what the world needed more than anything else; simple respect for the life of all creatures. Of course, the nefarious ones had to be controlled or eliminated. That was part and parcel of the messiness of the world. But otherwise, his motto was, *Let us all try to be nice to each other and respect the infinite complexity of every life, including our own.*

The old man had lived in Switzerland for almost five decades. He watched America from afar. In the summer of 2020, he watched George Floyd die and then he watched the protestors go into action. He wondered if they were aware of a few things. For example, according to the statistics he was able to find, as of July 29, 2020, a total of 558 civilians had been shot by police across the United States. 111 of these people were "Black". The others were labeled "White", "Hispanic", or "Other". The old man cared about all of them equally. How could he not? He didn't care what category they were thrown into. He knew the categories were absurd simplifications. (What were the *"Others"*? "Chinese"? "Swiss"? Lithuanian"? "Brownish-Green"? "Invisible"? "Pinkish-Beige"? "Alaskan with traces of Siberian"?) ... What a preposterous world he was living in! And then he wondered why nobody in America – from the 1st of January to the 29th of July – had protested any of the other shootings? Why had the 447 other people been shot by police and nobody had batted an eyelash? And then he wondered if the protestors knew that 84 police officers had been killed in America so far that year, and that 32 of them had been shot dead? Had anybody protested against *their* deaths?

The world was a three-ring circus with very little, if any, rhyme or reason.

Obviously all the horrors were horrendous. Obviously all the protesting had started after the George Floyd video had come out and gone viral. But one had to ask why it hadn't started long long before, when all these other people were being shot and killed and all the other horrors of the world were unfolding? Of course the answer was obvious: Because the news and social media had never picked up on the other stories, all of which were certainly just as horrible and tragic in one way or another as the George Floyd death. And what about the 27,000 Americans – many of them profoundly innocent – who had been shot by somebody during the first six months of the year 2020?

Were people *that* slow to be horrified by the shit in the world? Were their perspectives on life *that* limited?

The old man wanted the world to know that horrible things had been going on forever on this big ball of matter flying around the sun. Horrible shit. Always! All over the place involving all kinds of people and animals! There had always been tragic situations of unfairness, suffering, exploitation, and death going on around the world. The old man felt for all of them.

He thought it was wonderful that people were becoming aware of things. But these people were often blinded by simplistic explanations as to the causes of the horrors of the world. Most people had not studied or thought deeply about the world. They failed to think about the horrors of the world until the media pounded certain things into their eyes, ears, and brains. And then they simplified the causes instead of digging deeply.

The old man did not want to diminish the ugliness of what had happened to George Floyd or Jacob Blake or any person in the world. He just wanted the protestors to know that lots of so-called "Whites" and "Hispanics" and "Others" had also been shot and injured or killed by police officers and that many fine hard-working officers had also been shot and killed by malevolent people. He wanted protesters to do a little homework before they started taking to the streets.

The old man thought that only when *every* creature on earth was seen as unique, as infinitely complex, all "different" one from the other… only then would there be a chance for humanity to come together. Grouping people in "races" separated them into misleading categories warped any hope for truth and understanding. People needed to stop talking about **race** and start talking about **who** was truly kind and respectful of others and life! The world needed to go beyond race and into the heart of goodness. Only then would there be a real hope of creating a semblance of heaven on earth.

Of course the world would never be a paradise. This too had to be understood. Tragedy was built into the nature of existence. What was needed was simply more kindness and understanding than ever before.

Nietzsche proclaimed God's death. The old man proclaimed the death of Race. God's death gave this life supreme importance. The death of race would give supreme importance to all humans, and maybe one day even to all Being.

THE OLD MAN AND THE WOMAN

September 2, 2020

THE OLD MAN did not believe that the mind could be understood. He was an agnostic when it came to psychiatry and psychotherapy. Nonetheless, he didn't think the two fields were without merit because it was obvious that talking to someone who "cared about *you*" could certainly help a person get through the trials of living. He also felt there was no doubt that some of the drugs psychiatrists prescribed could definitely aid in reducing pain and anxiety. What the old man didn't believe was that a human mind could ever be truly comprehended or "understood" by itself or another human mind. He saw every moment of life to be infinitely complex, ephemeral, and hence unknowable. But that didn't mean he didn't play the game of trying to make a semblance of sense of things.

One such thing was his relationship with women.

The longer the old man lived the more it became apparent that most men form an image of *"women"* based on the experience they had with their own mothers. The same can be said of women forming an image of men based on their experience with their fathers. Throughout his life, the old man had noticed how women could be profoundly influenced by fathers who had seen them as sexual objects and "abused" them mentally, physically, or both, leaving deep scars on their daughters' weltanschauungs. He had also observed how an over-protective mother could render a son incapable of having "normal" relationships with a woman. And round and round the horses on the merry-go-round gallop...

What really fascinated the old man was how *his* mother had influenced his vision of the world and his relationships with women. She had been the most tender, gentle, caring woman he had ever known. She was never angry, never criticized others, and never yelled or screamed or scolded. She did everything with love and smiles. When the young (child) old man was feverish, she would rub alcohol on his body or hold a cool damp washcloth on his forehead. She would sit next to him on the bed, hold his hand, tell him how much she loved him, tuck him under the covers, and kiss him goodnight. She gave her life to making her family of seven happy. For the most part it worked.

The young old man grew up thinking all women were like his mother and that the world was a kind and gentle place. Of course it didn't take long for him to realize this was not the case. Nonetheless, when, as a young man, he went in search of love, there was one thing he always wanted... tenderness and sensuality. He craved those soft gentle hands on his body, on her body, and those delicate words and gestures of love in both minds. As love came and went and he got older, he never lost the deep desire for a sensual relationship with a woman. When such love and affection were absent for extended periods of time, his zest for life would be seriously affected, sometimes to the point where he would feel pushed to the brink of madness. He had often wondered if Hemingway had blown his brains out at age sixty-one simply because he felt he would never again feel profound reciprocal affection with a woman.

As the old man looked back at his life, he sensed there were two keys to how he felt about existence: first, the aforementioned relationship with his dear mother, and second, his religious education in a devout Mormon family. The two were tightly entwined. His mother was female perfection; the loving God he prayed to at night was male perfection. Yes, the God of his youth was definitely a male. And his mother was the Goddess of the universe. The two together gave him a sense of absolute meaning and an anointed place in the heart of Being.

When he lost his faith in the Mormon religion and the Mormon God, the only thing that was left was his mother, i.e. love with a woman. That was what kept him from losing his mind. The loss of God meant that all intellectual truth had been blown to smithereens. No god, no plan, no teleology, no sense, no built-in meaning and value. Humankind was on its own in an infinite futile cosmos. To save him from this madness, the old man counted on love. When love wasn't there, the void was.

The grand god and angelic mother of his youth had been both a blessing and a curse. Having been soaked in consummate love and the glorious tenet that everything in the universe made sense, when both were absent later in life, finding a reason to plow on had often been a hearty task. He reckoned that maybe that was why he had written so many books.

THE OLD MAN
AND THE PEACH TREE

September 4, 2020

WHEN THE OLD man was a baby his parents built a house with a big garden where they planted, among other things, a peach tree. By the time the old man was old enough to hit a baseball, the peach tree had grown to fruition. It produced real peaches that could be eaten in summer.

When the old man was young he completely took the peaches for granted. Today when he ate a peach he was astounded at the flavor, flesh, and juiciness of the piece of fruit that grew out of the ground. He was amazed that year after year trees could produce incredible amounts of apples, plums, oranges, lemons, limes, bananas, apricots, cherries, grapefruits, nectarines, pears, nuts, coconuts, mangos, and avocados.

Fruit, earth, water, tree! What wonderful parts of existence! As far as he knew, there were no fruit trees on Mars, or Saturn, or Jupiter, but there were millions of them on the earth, some right in our own back yards! The miracle of life was right in front of our noses! And how many of us were too dumb and blockheaded to appreciate what we had? The old man knew that he himself had been such a dimwit. He had lived for decades before truly appreciating a peach, a pear, an orange, or an apple, to say nothing of pomegranates or mangos.

Now, when the old man thought back to that peach tree in

Orinda, California, he felt like the greatest sinner alive. He had committed the sin of non-appreciation. He had been guilty of taking things for granted. He thought he should be consigned to the depths of Hades for not recognizing the miracle of all that existed around him. Everything was mind-blowing. This he knew now that he was an old man. Why had it taken him so long? Was it his fault? Was he really an evildoer? Was a slow brain an excuse?

As he thought about the peach tree in the garden, he thought about people everywhere and at all times in the history of the world. Who appreciated the world? Who loved the world? Who hated the world? Were there more lovers or haters? ... But did any of this really matter? Weren't all the people just as miraculous, strange, and wondrous as the fruit in the garden? And then which was more amazing, a person or the brain inside the person? Or the brain or the heart? Or the tree or the peach? The peach or the pit? The mouth or the tongue? The god or the kingdom? The love or the lovers? The proton or the electron?

As he thought these kinds of things, sometimes the old man laughed out loud.

THE OLD MAN AND THE EDUCATED PEOPLE

September 10, 2020

THE OLD MAN knew there were many *many* uneducated people. But was the opposite also true? Were there many *many* educated people?

The answer naturally depended on one's definition of "educated". Did being able to read and write coupled with the ability to add, subtract, multiply and divide mean one was educated? The old man remembered back to his youthful days in California when he and his friends were given long serious tests in English and Math and then were compared with other students across the country. They were usually in the top five percentile. Did that mean they were educated? It certainly was supposed to make them proud. Most likely it just showed they were lucky…

Does having a university degree make one educated? Does reading a lot of books or knowing a truckload of "facts" do the trick?

When he was young, the old man thought there were a lot of educated people in the world. The longer he lived the more the number had dwindled.

Why? Because for him a truly "educated person" was someone who didn't look at the world with fixed ideas about things (things like *truth, reality, causality, morality, stars, worms, language, cats, minds, mice, trumps, bidens, birds, history, love, etc.*) but rather looked at existence with constant wonder and openness. As he got older, it seemed to the old man that – in the end – education tended to close minds more than open them. "Educated" people seemed inclined to think they really knew what the hell they were talking about when it came to things like truth, reality, causality, morality, stars, worms, language, cats, minds, mice, trumps, bidens, birds, history, love, etc. So sure were they of their vision of the world that the old man often felt they should rather be placed in the opposite category, i.e. the uneducated, or at least the *under*educated.

Proof of this was that rarely did the old man see people change their minds about things. Rarely did he see people who doubted their own convictions and beliefs. Rarely did he see people who walked gently, reflected before they spoke or judged, and who regarded the world with awe, reverence, astonishment, and broad-mindedness. Rarely did he encounter people who dug deeply into ontological, epistemological, and ethical problems. Rarely did he meet people who saw the complexity of all things. This, he thought, was what truly *educated* people did. But most people seemed cemented for life in their beliefs about what the world was and how it worked. He wondered if, in their own way, humans weren't actually part of the crustacean species, an out-of-water kind of shelled creature stuck in its hard intellectual crust for life.

Let it be clear, the old man knew that there was another kind of "education" that worked extremely well in the world, i.e. the kind that taught people to build bridges, washing machines, computers, telephones, cars, airplanes, roads, hospitals, rocket ships, tanks, skyscrapers, nuclear arms, and Lego kits. He greatly appreciated many of these things and the people who created them…

But in this case he was talking about another kind of

education... the kind that might one day stop wars, jingoism, political pettiness, racial and tribal-territorial ignorance, marital bickering, street violence, and which might allow human beings to live together with a global appreciation of the miracle of being alive. If and when such a day came he was sure he would then freely admit that lots and lots of people were truly worthy of their caps and gowns.

THE OLD MAN AND THE SQUASH

September 13, 2020

WHEN THE OLD man was a young boy growing up in California in the rolling hills east of Oakland, he hated squash. They were seven in the house and he was the only one of them who wouldn't eat the zucchini that his dear mother grew in the garden. He otherwise was a great eater of vegetables – things like peas, carrots, string beans, broccoli, lettuce, beets (he wasn't called "Beetle Bomb" for nothing), onions, potatoes, and tomatoes were all among his favorite foods. His mother used to tell him that he was the only child she's ever seen who preferred salad to dessert and who would eat lettuce and carrots for an afternoon snack. But there was something about squash that left his taste buds cold and, as he used to say, made him *"want to throw up"*.

Today the old man loved squash. Last night he fried some for dinner with garlic, onions, herbs, and canned tomatoes and he had three helpings.

So what happened? What made the old man change his mind about that long hard dark-green vegetable? What had been behind his youthful prejudice and his culinary metamorphosis later in life? Had his mind changed? His tongue? His vision of the food? Had he finally "grown up"?

When he was about fifty he asked himself why he didn't eat

squash. It couldn't be the taste because squash really had little or no taste at all. He finally came to the conclusion that silly childish predilection probably just started because of the name of the vegetable, i.e. "squash". When his young mind heard the word it had visions of crushed insects, dogs and cats hit by cars, and any number of "squashed" things that were disgusting and ugly and certainly not to be "eaten".

In any case, he realized that his dislike of squash had no rational logic to it. And yet it had lasted for five decades. How could he have held such a prejudice for so long? He decided it was because he had an idiot side to his being. He could be stupid and irrational.

Today, as an old man observing the world through both a telescope and a microscope, he wondered if all human beings had an idiot side... *Doesn't everyone have silly infantile prejudices that are not rooted in serious reflection, but are as arbitrary and unfounded as his hatred of the zucchini family?...* He pondered.

He watched the 2020 presidential campaign. There were intelligent people on all sides of the fence. There were intelligent people who hated Trump. There were intelligent people who disliked Biden. There were intelligent pro-Biden people and intelligent pro-Trumpers. *(If you don't agree with this,* the old man thought, *you are incurably stuck in your mindset.)* The situation was not simple; in fact the race for the White House and state of the world was infinitely complex. And yet there were millions of people who were **categorically** anti-Trump or anti-Biden, as categorical as the old man had been in his hate for squash. Were these people stupid people, as stupid as he had been as a boy in California?

Hence, the old man couldn't help wondering if lifelong die-hard Republicans and lifelong die-hard Democrats were not just as irrationally closed-minded as he had been about squash.

Weren't there valid arguments on almost all sides of the political spectrum? Weren't simplistic explanations often touted on all sides? Where really was "the good"? Did anyone know? Surely men like Trump and Biden, who had come this far in life, couldn't be all good or all bad?

The old man liked to ask questions about what he saw in the world and about the evolution of his own predilections and prejudices.

He had hated squash, now he loved squash. But, for some inane reason, at age seventy he still couldn't put a piece of egg in his mouth without gagging on it.

THE OLD MAN AND THE FIRES

September 13, 2020

THE WILD WEST was burning, especially California. The old man watched from ten thousand kilometers away. He remembered how it never rained in the East Bay from June to the end of September. His father had wanted to raise his family there because of the weather. Though sent to Baltimore as an FBI agent during World War II, they – the father and mother – moved back to Oakland where the old man was born. When the old man was a year old, the family moved fifteen miles east to Orinda, far from the madding crowd and where the air temperature was always a few degrees warmer.

Millions of other people had similar ideas. California became the place to be. It had everything. Hollywood, Disneyland, Newport Beach, Sequoia forests, Lake Tahoe, Death Valley, cable cars, the Dodgers and Giants, the Central Valley, Carmel, Muir Woods, Mount Shasta. And the weather was unbeatable.

California grew. The earthquakes and the Andreas fault didn't keep people away. Nor did the fires. When they were burning in 2020 there were close to 40,000,000 people living in the state.

What is fire? Is it a friend or foe? Is the sun not a ball of fire? Without it we would all be frozen. Actually we wouldn't be. For thousands – maybe millions – of years, we cooked with fire. We warmed our bodies and abodes with fire. Wherever it was cold, we were thankful for fire.

These days in California people hate fire. It is the enemy. Whose fault is this? Ours or fire's?

The old man's brother's house had burned down in the fire in a place called "Paradise". He lost everything except his wife and car and two suitcases full of clothes. They had been on vacation when that fire destroyed 90% of the town. They left California and moved to Idaho.

People around San Francisco were complaining about fire. Smoke had made the sky orange at eleven o'clock in the morning. Big fires were bad. These ones were big.

The Wild West was burning.

THE OLD MAN AND THE LAST WORD

September 16, 2020

THE OLD MAN felt the time was coming to shut up. He had perhaps said enough, nearly 40,000 words herein. He had often wondered why he kept on writing… more than thirty books; more than a million words. The best answer he could come up with was that it allowed himself somebody to talk to. When he read what he had written the day – or week or month or years – before, at least he had somebody to communicate with. He tended to agree with himself. He had a friend in himself. There weren't a lot of other people with whom he felt a shared vision of existence. He wondered if that came out in this book, *The Old Man and the Stone*.

Yes, soul mates were so hard to come by.

The old man had often said, *"Nothing can be other than what it is"*. He had rarely explained what this idea meant for himself and for his vision of the world. That explanation would be some of his last words:

Nothing in the universe can be other that what it is…

The thought is extremely difficult to fathom. It is a kind of "last word" because when you feel (to the bone) that nothing – absolutely nothing – can be other that what it is, your old vision of life will disappear forever. Every "thing" you see in existence will cease to exist. There will be no things. All concreteness will vanish. There will be no more "Trump" to criticize, no "Biden" to make fun of, no "eagle", no "mouse", no "atom" or "electron" or "quark" to identify, and there will be no "today", "tomorrow", or "yesterday". All Being will be tied together and all will be in constant flux. Nothing will be *fixed* and hence nothing can be "talked about". It will all be gone as soon as it comes to be. All will be ethereal, and hence impossible to make sense of.

Most human beings cannot grasp this idea because it goes against everything they think and do. Their whole lives they have been taught to break existence into pieces and to make sense of it (and to think they have made sense of it... and for themselves, *they have*). They separate everything, give names to everything, think they see causal relationships happening between all the "things" they have identified, believe in beginnings and ends, believe their *fixed identifiable* things are "real" things, and once they have "their view of the world", they tend to stick with it for life. A tree is a tree. A dog is a dog. A Trump is a Trump. A country is a country. An atom is an atom. You are you. I am me. And *"that's the way things are!"*

But none of these things are fixed things. They are constantly changing. All parts of existence are constantly changing. The whole of existence is constantly changing. Existence is a great swirl. It has no beginning and no end.

This can be the last word. Given that there are no fixed things, all judgments about "things" are erroneous. All judgments about things are purely human constructions that have nothing to do with reality. Reality can never be identified because it is always in flux. We can never know reality. We are part of the great swirl. Our reality is not real reality. It never has been and it never will be. We are simply those creatures who decided we could *"know"* things. But we don't, because there are no things to know. And every bit of being is what it is at any given moment and can be nothing other than what it is. Absolutely nothing in the entire universe can be other than what it is forever and ever and ever. Here, we are not knocking on heaven's door, but on infinity's door, and infinity is deeper – much deeper – than human minds can grasp, or even hope to entertain. We groveling humans are to the universe what crabs crawling on the bottom of the ocean are to the earth. We have no clue as to what *Being* really is.

The human race and all its cares are but a tiny muffled heartbeat in the infinite cosmic swirl. Nothing is free. Nothing is determined. Everything simply is what it is at every given instant and every instant is gone as soon as it happens.

When one feels this kind of thing, one finds very few people with whom to share the world... This, the last word?

Almost.

THE OLD MAN AND THE STORY

November 23, 2020

*C**AN WE NOT understand, the old man wondered, that every human being has a unique story to tell? Millions, billions, trillions of "bodies" composed of "organs" and who-knows-what. Millions, billions, trillions of "minds" composed of more who-knows-what. Brains, skin, blood, bladders, mouths, eyes, ears, lungs, hearts, fingers, feet, intestines, anuses, and all the rest all over the planet. And each body and mind has a story... Ah! There's a holy trinity for you: Body, Mind, and Story!* The old man laughed.

What could be more beautiful than the idea that every single solitary human being has a unique story, an interesting story, a true story, a real "life" story? *But wait!* the old man thought, *I have an even better idea. What if we all "respected" every individual's story? Can you imagine that... a world wherein everybody respects – and even tries to "understand" – the uniqueness of every other person and every other person's story? Can you imagine that?* The old man did a little jitterbug with his feet in his old worn-out shoes.

And then the old man had the crowning thought: What if every human being not only respected the life and story of all *people*, but also of all *living creatures*, i.e. all animals and plants. But then the old man had a little chill go down his spine and he thought that the whole of existence was a *living creature*. How could something exist and not be "alive"? Just because something wasn't alive like a person was alive didn't mean that it wasn't alive! The old man thought about the chief in the film "Little Big Man" and how he said that the difference between the "human beings" (the Indians) and the "white man" was that for the Indians everything was alive and hence to be respected. The white man only respected what he needed for himself.

The old man thought a bit more... *But no story is really "true". No story is ever the "whole" story. Every story is partial. None of us can ever know or remember everything about anybody, including ourselves. When we look back at our own story, the mind flashes a few selected memories, a few moments that get woven together to try to tell us who we are and what we have done. But so much has been forgotten. So much is lost forever. If a person cannot ever know his or her own story, how can he or she be expected to fully grasp someone else's story?*

The old man wondered how many people realized how true this was. All the books in the world could never tell the real story of any human being – or anything else for that matter. *We are all mysteries to ourselves and each other.*

The old man scratched his head. On the one hand he wanted every creature's story to be told and respected. On the other hand he knew all stories were partial and that real truth could never be told. *Never ever can you understand another life – or even your own. Is this a tragedy or a blessing?* The old man pondered.

THE OLD MAN AND THE WOMAN WITH WHOM HE LIVES

June 14, 2021

THE OLD MAN and the woman have lived together for twenty-one years. They share a house, meals, vacations, a daughter, a cat, and two rabbits. Three dogs and two other rabbits were part of the family until they died. The dogs were what brought the man and the woman together. They met in the forest walking with their pets.

When they met, the old man had recently divorced and the woman had recently split with her boyfriend after years of trying to produce a child. The old man and the younger woman began talking and enjoying each other's company. The dogs got along well, too. They were all sterilized and so there was no lovemaking between them. Not so for the humans. After they made love a few good times with protection against offspring, they decided they would live together and maybe even have a child. They did both. That was back then.

Since another part of back then the woman doesn't want to be touched by the old man. They still sleep in the same bed but there is a demilitarized zone in the middle where any crossing results in a foot kick or hand tap. What happened was that the old man did something more than a decade ago that caused a cessation of tactile exchange between them. The old man seems to be the only one who suffers from a lack of bodily contact. This morning as he was lying in bed next to the woman, he thought that the only time he would be able to touch her without getting whacked would be when she was dead. The idea saddened him greatly because he was still fond of her. Given she was fourteen years younger than the old man, the odds were stacked against him ever touching her again.

THE OLD MAN AND THE LETTER

November 25, 2021

THEY LIVED IN a house. Part of the "they" was a cat named Tilou that we'll call "T". The abode was interestingly situated between the train tracks and the freeway, a fact that had done wonders for making the place affordable for a recently divorced man (we'll call him "He") in a region where a cup of coffee exchanged for roughly four dollars and real estate was up there with the earth's most desired (the area was known as "Suisse," "Schweiz" or "Svizzera", "Switzerland", etc. depending on where one was). Another reason He had bought the house was the decent-sized fenced-in garden. When He and C first met, C had one dog and He had two. When they moved into the house the dogs were robust and the garden was a godsend, except when the hounds tracked in mud and such (then it became disputed territory). Now… then… twenty years later, the dogs were long gone, but T, when not sprawling in one of his favorite spots, had turned the garden into his own private killing field. Mice, of course, were his victims of predilection, though over the years he had ended life for a few lizards and birds and at least one snake.

Like many angels of prey, T slept during the day and prowled at night. A few years prior He and C had a special window put in allowing T to come and go as he pleased. They hadn't foreseen that this would allow T to bring his catches into the house, consistently leaving what was left of a victim on a carpeted step equidistant between their bedroom on the ground floor and their daughter's bedroom upstairs. They supposed this was T's way of showing that he loved them equally.

When T came into the house in the middle of the night with a warm body between his jaws, the animal was not always dead. After announcing his arrival with horrid guttural sounds, T would sometimes play with his prey, i.e. bat it around on the fake wooden floor in the hall as if it were a hockey puck. Occasionally a creature would escape and hide. One time neither T nor He nor C had been able to find the critter. It turned out it that had been hiding in His gym bag, which He never zipped up and always left on the floor in the bedroom. They knew this because a couple of days later, as He was driving to His fitness club, a mouse – *the* mouse – scurried past the arm that was settled on the armrest. It scared the pucky out of Him, but He quickly realized that it was the mouse they had been looking for. Catching it in the car took another two days. C bought a special trap-cage, a brilliant invention that lured the mouse inside (usually a tiny piece of cheese did the trick) and when the food was touched the door snapped shut. The mouse would be caught (certainly after being scared shitless by the sound of the slamming portal), but not killed. Neither C nor He was capable of killing a fly.

About a year ago C found something amazing on the step (which the family had labeled "Tilou's Cemetery"): a fetus in a bloody nest of guts. It seems T had eaten the pregnant mother, but left her baby untouched. *Yes,* He imagined, *T has a heart after all.* A year prior He had written this poem:

The Heart

No one knows what happens in the heart.
The heart, like all existence, is a great mystery.
I do not own my heart; if anything, my heart owns me.
My heart will stop beating when it wants to, not when I want it to, unless I shoot myself in the head or get hit by a train or some such rigmarole.
One night in bed many years ago I realized that my heart was not attached to anything like a power generator or a battery. It just beats. And beats. And beats. It has no outside help. From that night on I understood that my heart is as special as the universe. It just is.
I don't think the heart has anything to do with love,
except that no one knows what happens in love either.
Most hearts beat much longer than most loves, and much more steadily.
Without a heart you die. The same cannot be said for a love.
As I have aged, being loved has become less important than having a heart.
I recently asked a biologist if worms have hearts. They do, she said, but their hearts are shaped differently and their blood is not like our blood.
So what? I thought. A heart is a heart. Blood is blood.
My cat has killed ten mice in the last six days. They have hearts, those mice, and crimson blood.
Tilou is a serial killer with a heart.
No one knows what happens in the heart.

The fetus didn't survive of course, except in a picture C took of it. But T had left it whole and immaculate. C said it had been about the size of a baby's thumb.

This brings world history to something that occurred last week when T's prey escaped and eventually hid in a heap of large sticks that He had recently gathered and placed next to the chimney. After a couple of days C heard some noise coming from the stack of sticks. She investigated and found a little nest with two baby mice inside, both alive and moving. The mother was not there, having probably skedaddled when she sensed a human presence in the vicinity. C reset the special life-sparing trap and eventually caught the mother. C and He hadn't wanted a family of mice roaming the house. C put the three mice outside in the garden in a box-sized house that they had once used for rabbits. First she took the two babies, then the mother. To C's surprise, when she opened the cage-trap and released the mother next to her babies, it immediately bolted the scene and disappeared. When C came back a few hours later to check on the babies, they were gone. C and He comforted themselves by surmising that the mother had found a better home for her family and that the three mice were safe and sound somewhere.

C had taken a picture of the two babies before transporting them to the garden. Though she was a nurse – or because she was a nurse – she was an extremely sensitive woman, but also had a tough stoic side. When He (the old man) looked at the picture of the two baby mice, He wondered if it was their mutual respect for all creatures that had brought them together two decades prior. Since then, in spite of the fact that both still could not kill a spider or a fly, their relationship had deteriorated to the point that she had not touched Him in more than ten years. As stated before, whenever He tried to touch C she would move away and/or slap His hand. Whenever He tried to talk to her about their relationship (remember, they still slept in the same bed), she would blow Him off and say, "Oh, not that again."

After the incident with the baby mice, He decided it was a good time to write a letter to C....

Dear C,

Given that you don't like to discuss things, I decided I would take this opportunity to write you after watching you be so loving and tender with the baby mice and their mother.

I think both of us are kind and loving people who share a profound respect for "life". So, I ask myself, why is it that we share no love for each other? Of course I know that things happen in life that can make two people change their feelings about each other. In our case, I did things that affected you in a certain way. For more than ten years now you haven't touched me and you certainly haven't wanted me to touch you. Yes, during that decade, there have been moments when I found other people who wanted to touch me and I was able to live reasonably happily and not lose my mind. I don't know if you yourself have had a physical relation with anyone, other than the hugging and tenderness you share with our dear daughter. I of course, as a father, am not allowed the same kind of caresses. I understand and respect that.

For a few years now, I have had absolutely nobody to touch or hold in my arms. For someone like myself – someone who loves sensual moments – this has been extremely difficult to bear. I have often felt an acute loneliness and isolation.

I never want anyone to do things against her or his will. Never would I want you to "love me" if you felt no desire to do so. But I think you loved me once, at least you cared for me enough to want to touch me and live together and have a child together. So I would like to see if by asking for your forgiveness for whatever I have done in the past, that maybe we could come to a point we could share a certain tenderness again. I think humans need to be touched and need a touch of tenderness. In my experience I know I am happier when I can share feelings and share joy with someone I care about. And I do care about you. I have lived with you longer than with any other person on earth. If there is no way for us to share moments of tenderness again, then so be it. I will accept it like I have accepted these last years. But I would still like to try to see if we can forgive and forget and feel the same innocence and compassion for each other that we have for Tilou and all his victims. I firmly believe that men and women are as innocent as mice and cats. All do what they do and can do nothing other. We all prefer some people to others... that's for sure. I do think we still each have a lot of likeable things about us.

Sincerely and hopefully,

The Old Man

THE OLD MAN AND THE SUPERFLUOUS

November 30, 2021

THE OLD MAN loved the word *"superfluous"*. The synonyms were many and, he thought, glorious – even themselves superfluous: *excessive, expendable, gratuitous, surplus, redundant, unneeded, not required, extra, extravagant, exorbitant, extreme, inessential, inordinate, lavish, abounding, de trop, spare, remaining, inessential, overflowing, needless, supernumerary, pleonastic, profuse, useless, unproductive, undue, surplus, overmuch, dispensable, unwanted, unasked, uncalled-for, waste...*

As he looked at all the words ("pleonastic" was his favorite) his mind wandered and wondered about what in this world fit smack dab into the category of superfluity in Western civilization. Where was the love of life, the feeling of mystery, and the sense of awe over the simple fact of existence?

Then he thought of what else there was *not* too much of in the world: kindness, love, respect for existence in general and in particular, reflection, perspective, patience, moderation, fresh food, good wine, people who drive carefully, people who appreciate being alive, people who walk softly, etc.

He thought of Seneca, Epictetus, and Marcus Aurelius and compared them to the politicians we listened to today.

The old man was not sentimental about the past. He knew the flow of existence was beyond him and out of his control. The

Stoics knew it too. But people these days didn't seem to know it. They talked like the world was made for them and they became angry if things weren't the way they wanted them to be.

The old man was probably tired as he thought about all the superfluity and the state of the world. Surely fatigue had affected his mood. But he knew that sooner or later he would see that – when all was said and done – there were two possibilities: *either everything was superfluous or nothing was superfluous*. And he knew his mind would always go with the latter. Why? Because if he was convinced of one thing in life, it was that nothing – absolutely nothing – could be other than what it was.

Enjoyed this book? Let others know through an online review.
The Old Man and the Stone is also available in illustrated Kindle format.

BOOKS BY JON FERGUSON

(Published by Huge Jam)

Adam's Cane
Foster's Depression
The Last Day Forever
Jesus & Mary
Mary & God
God & Naomi
The Flood
The Anthropologist
Three Forgotten Tales

Out soon by the same author:

Nietzsche for Breakfast
Burnt Roses
Lucie's Tomb
Don't Bullshit Me Daddy

www.hugejam.com
www.jonfergusonbooks.com

ABOUT THE AUTHOR

Jon Ferguson was born in October 1949 in Oakland, California, into a devout Christian family, much like his favorite philosopher, Friedrich Nietzsche. In fact, as a child, church services were held in the family living room. At age 17, his passion for sport was almost usurped by a keenness to save the world when he enrolled at the Mormon-owned Brigham Young University. Little by little, though, he realized that if Jesus couldn't do it, neither could he. His faith in divinity began to crumble. With an adieu to the US academic world where he'd been immersed in anthropology and philosophy – and with a desire to engage with the world at large – Ferguson hopped on a plane in 1973 and by chance ended up in Nyon, Switzerland where he was soon playing basketball in the top Swiss league, becoming a key player in what fans consider to have been the golden age.

Half a century later, still in Switzerland, he is now just as well known for his writing (eighteen books published in French) as for his coaching (thirty years' worth). He won more games than any coach in Swiss basketball history, but he likes to remind people that he lost more than everyone else as well... He has written over twenty novels and a book on Nietzsche, Nietzsche au Petit Déjeuner ("Nietzsche for Breakfast") and a book on the history of Swiss basketball, Of Hoops and Men. For twenty-five years he also wrote a bi-weekly column in the Lausanne newspaper called "Ainsi Parla Schmaltz". His novel Farley's Jewel (Cinco Puntos Press, 1998) won a Barnes & Noble "Discover Great New Writers of America" prize.

Find out more:
www.jonfergusonbooks.com

www.ingramcontent.com/pod-product-compliance
Lightning Source LLC
Chambersburg PA
CBHW072055110526
44590CB00018B/3180